Praise for *Forget the Fairy Tale and Find Your Happiness*

"Pure magic! Deb Miller's story is proof that we live our best lives when we refuse to settle for less than we deserve. Inspiring and powerful; every woman should read this."

—**Jill Zarin, author, entrepreneur, and original cast member of** *The Real Housewives of New York City*

"*Forget the Fairy Tale & Find Your Happiness* is a hopeful memoir about claiming ownership over one's life."

—*Foreword Clarion Reviews*

"In Miller's inspiring account of finding happiness outside of societal expectations, she reminds readers—and herself—that 'my happiness is up to me.'"

—**BookLife Reviews**

"Deb Miller's extraordinary and invaluable insights guide women toward finding happiness by rejecting societal expectations and not depending on men to be heroes on white horses."

—**Jack Zipes, Professor Emeritus at the University of Minnesota, and author of** *Fairy Tales and the Art of Subversion and Breaking the Magic Spell*

"Although women have come a long way, they still need to hear the wisdom in Miller's story: be the CEO of your own life."

—**Bonnie Comfort, author of** *Staying Married is the Hardest Part*

"Brilliantly weaving her own courageous story with those of fairytale princesses, Miller cleverly winds through decades of pain, joy, heartbreak and healing. I could not put down this glorious memoir."

—**Marty Ross-Dolen, author of *Always There, Always Gone***

"Written with honesty, depth, and courage, Deb Miller's engaging memoir is a cautionary tale for all ages. Many readers will identify with her struggle against the pervasive pull of cultural expectation and be inspired to chart their own life's path."

—**Dianne Ebertt Beeaff, author of *Infinite Paradise***

"Beautifully told, Deb Miller's story illustrates the shift from dependence to strength and self-reliance. It offers an entertaining and thought-provoking reflection on how societal expectations shape both fictional princesses and real women. I highly recommend this captivating read."

—**Jelaine Lombardi, author of *Running Around Naked***

"A passionate and engaging read."

—**Jude Berman, author of *The Die* and *The Vow***

"With humor, heart, and a keen eye for cultural commentary, Miller's narrative shines as a beacon for those embracing life's complexities and chasing authentic joy."

—**Kristina Amelong, author of *What My Brother Knew***

"I love how Miller braided the evolution of the Disney princesses with her own evolution. What a life she has had! Fun read. Inspiring and uplifting."

—**Lisa Cheek, author of *Sit, Cinderella, Sit***

"With humor, heart, and unflinching honesty, this book is an invitation to every woman to rewrite her own story and find the courage to live authentically. If you've ever questioned the script society handed you, this book will inspire you to let it go and write your own."

—**Keri Wilt, host of *The Well-Tended Life* podcast and historical lecturer about her great-great grandmother, Frances Hodgson Burnett**

"An engaging and rollicking ride!"

—**Suzanne Parry, author of *Lost Souls of Leningrad***

"A modern-day fairy tale that will empower little girls for generations to come! Bravo!"

—**Rossana D'Antonio, author of *26 Seconds***

FORGET
THE
Fairy Tale
AND
FIND YOUR
Happiness

FORGET THE *Fairy Tale* AND FIND YOUR *Happiness*

DEB MILLER

SHE WRITES PRESS

Copyright © 2025, Deb Miller

All rights reserved. No part of this publication may be reproduced, distributed, or transmitted in any form or by any means, including photocopying, recording, digital scanning, or other electronic or mechanical methods, without the prior written permission of the publisher, except in the case of brief quotations embodied in critical reviews and certain other noncommercial uses permitted by copyright law. For permission requests, please address She Writes Press.

Published 2025
Printed in the United States of America
Print ISBN: 978-1-64742-922-5
E-ISBN: 978-1-64742-923-2
Library of Congress Control Number: 2024927051

For information, address:
She Writes Press
1569 Solano Ave #546
Berkeley, CA 94707

Interior Design by Andrea Reider

She Writes Press is a division of SparkPoint Studio, LLC.

Company and/or product names that are trade names, logos, trademarks, and/or registered trademarks of third parties are the property of their respective owners and are used in this book for purposes of identification and information only under the Fair Use Doctrine.

NO AI TRAINING: Without in any way limiting the author's [and publisher's] exclusive rights under copyright, any use of this publication to "train" generative artificial intelligence (AI) technologies to generate text is expressly prohibited. The author reserves all rights to license uses of this work for generative AI training and development of machine learning language models.

Names and identifying characteristics have been changed to protect the privacy of certain individuals.

100% author-written

Dedication

Love and miss you, Mom.
Still down here trying to make you proud.

For Hadley, Tyler, and Ally,
who made my happily ever after possible.

"All women are princesses, it is our right."

—Frances Hodgson Burnett, *A Little Princess*

Table of Contents

Prologue	xiii
Section I—Someday My Prince Will Come	**1**
Chapter 1—To the Ball After All	3
Chapter 2—Royal Coupling	11
Chapter 3—Following Tradition	19
Section II—Living the Dream	**31**
Chapter 4—Once Upon a Time	33
Chapter 5—Time Flies	39
Chapter 6—My Royal Family	54
Chapter 7—White Horses	74
Section III—A Whole New World	**89**
Chapter 8—The Russians Are Coming	91
Chapter 9—Have Passport, Will Travel	108
Chapter 10—Back Home in Indiana	125
Chapter 11—Going Global	140

Section IV—Something There — 157

Chapter 12—Prince Charming — 159
Chapter 13—Hello, It's Me — 173
Chapter 14—Russian Hotel — 192
Chapter 15—Three's a Charm and Four's an Alarm — 207

Section V—I Will Ride — 227

Chapter 16—Finding the Courage — 229
Chapter 17—Finding the Truth — 248
Chapter 18—My True Loves — 267
Chapter 19—Mirror, Mirror on the Wall — 277

Epilogue — 281

Author's Note

The stories in this book reflect the author's recollection of events. Some names, locations, and identifying characteristics have been changed to protect the privacy of those depicted.

Disclaimer

The opinions, interpretations, and views expressed in this memoir regarding Disney and its characters, including any references to Disney Princesses, are solely my own. They do not represent, reflect, or claim to be endorsed by The Walt Disney Company or any of its affiliates. Any analysis or commentary on Disney's works is intended for personal reflection and should not be construed as the official stance of The Walt Disney Company.

Prologue

Fairy tales about damsels in distress, their dashing male rescuers, and happy endings have been around for centuries. We can't blame Disney for inventing this path for women; it merely added animation and catchy soundtracks to the lessons women had been taught.

January 2000

It would take days for my shoulders to relax after clutching the wheel and hunching over to see out the frosty windshield of my brand-new 1999 Honda Accord. It was one of those tricky driving days when Mother Nature tests your patience and driving skills. My long commute had begun in fog and sleet, but the temperature dropped rapidly as I drove, and heavy snow was in the forecast. On days like this, I questioned the sanity of my decision to commute more than a hundred miles round trip to keep my family in the burbs, where they enjoyed strong schools and sports programs. That left me driving daily to the small town in Southern Indiana where I grew up and now worked. But today's dangerous wintry drive was not my average commute. I usually cruised the highway at seventy-five miles an hour while checking items off my to-do list. However, I wouldn't multitask on the phone to arrange the kids' schedules or conduct conference calls with Europe this morning. But my brain still found space to wander, and I thought about him.

He'd been gone for about three months now. Maybe it was time to tell people he wasn't coming back. I'd been hiding the truth, sure he'd show up again—worried that if I shared news of his departure, people wouldn't accept him if he returned. Maybe they'd been right about him all along. What kind of husband abandons his wife and child—and moves across the country? My dad never would have left his family. He took care of us. That's what real men did.

Still foggy, the rain turned into bits of ice about halfway through my commute, and the wipers struggled to keep a clear view. If only I could've stayed home today, but as a single mom, the whole family depended on me. My grip on the wheel relaxed as I reached my exit—one last mile. I slowed to a crawl as the sleet became a snowy blizzard. The wind whipped across the open fields, and I felt ice forming on the two-lane road that led to my office parking lot and safety. An oncoming car whizzed past, going dangerously fast for the conditions. I shook my head and inched toward the river crossing, the final hurdle between my office and me. Just before the bridge, I hit black ice and lost control. Dad taught me not to panic or hit the brakes on ice. But even that lesson couldn't stop my slide toward the bridge and a horrific conclusion.

The snowy windshield framed three snapshots as my car continued to slide. The first was a red oncoming vehicle. The black ice took my car directly into its path. We were about to collide head-on. Just then, a second image, the solid wall of the concrete bridge. I was going to hit the bridge instead. But no, my vehicle veered off the road at the last moment. The third snapshot was the dark and swirling river just ahead of me. Then everything went black.

SECTION 1

Someday My Prince Will Come

Many young baby boomers like me initially accepted society's directive that "a woman's place is in the home." We imagined that someday our prince would come, and together, we'd live happily ever after. We wouldn't require an actual prince, and the white horse was optional. The guy merely needed to provide for the family and generate the woman's happiness.

Snow White was the first Disney princess to follow that traditional princess path. The movie's opening song was set at a wishing well where Snow White outlined her plan to let a man "find" her. It seemed simple enough. No wonder Snow fell for the first guy who kissed her.

CHAPTER 1

To the Ball After All

With a little help from her friends, this rags-to-riches protagonist stepped out of a pumpkin carriage to explore life beyond the confines of home. She met a prince at the party and enjoyed a magical dance in the moonlight. Spoiler alert: There may be a shoe lost in the process.

Lesson 1—Follow the Path

Occasionally, my sister, Teresa, and I got to stay up past bedtime and watch a movie on the family's black-and-white television with foil on the antennae. In 1965, it was Lesley Ann Warren in Rodgers and Hammerstein's *Cinderella*. Cinderella's fantasy was my mom's reality. I believed it would also be my key to success—my princess path to a good life. The moms in my neighborhood seemed to follow a similar journey. Brief college stays long enough to land a guy and become a stay-at-home wife and mom.

Forget the Fairy Tale and Find Your Happiness

Mom explained an updated version of the plan: "Nobody wants to end up an old maid, so girls need to find a husband. It used to only take about one year of college. But *nowadays*, the girls graduate." She rattled off a list of neighbor girls who had completed that schedule. "So *your* father has to pay for you two girls to go to college, not just for our two boys. That means four kids for four years each, which is a lot of money! You girls should be grateful."

That's when I first understood that girls *could* expect to go to college—and to graduate! From that moment on, I understood my precise path—I was supposed to go to college and get an education, but I should find a husband during my four-year stay. That's how I'd reach my happily ever after to become a mom!

It was 1975 and move-in day for me and 35,000 other college students at Purdue University. The last day my hair would smell stale, like secondhand smoke. The last day I'd have to endure the prisonlike rules I followed while living with my parents. Dad held his cigarette near the cracked window; occasionally, he'd take a long drag and exhale in the general direction of the opening. No one spoke during the three-hour drive. The shrill whistle from the lone window filled the silence.

Our dog, Puff, awoke in the back seat and stood on her hind legs next to me. With her nose pressed against the window, she must've sensed something worth watching besides the flat, endless fields of corn and soybeans. We passed the county courthouse, crossed the Wabash River, and joined a long line of cars. The final stretch of our journey was a slow crawl up the town's only hill and through the gateway to Purdue's campus. Students walking on the packed sidewalks moved faster than the cars.

My heart beat almost as loudly as the music pounding from fraternity house windows. With all this traffic, my life would have to wait a little longer to begin. In a few minutes, Mom would drop off her youngest child at college and complete her mission of motherhood. But I doubted Mom would experience maternal feelings—even at this landmark moment. I was the youngest of her four children. When my oldest brother left, Mom cried for weeks and Dad became the parent president of his fraternity. But ten years later, they were bored with raising children.

My dorm, Fowler Courts, was a row of converted army barracks built before I was born. Only one story high and with a flat roof, the buildings stood in contrast to other new, tall, glistening dorms, but to me, it was heaven. Dad landed an ideal parking spot near the entrance to my new home, and I slipped on Puff's leash. By the time Dad opened the trunk, Puff had watered the parched grass, and I'd already assured my parents I could take it from there. I'd miss Puff but couldn't wait to see my high school friends on campus, and those I was about to meet. I didn't need my parents' help hauling my possessions for the last few yards and assumed Mom wouldn't want the humidity to mess up her hairstyle. Dad would be anxious to start the long drive back. "See you at Thanksgiving," was all we said. I guess that sums up where we were after eighteen years together. Turning to conceal my smile, I inhaled my first wonderful breath of freedom.

Forget the Fairy Tale and Find Your Happiness

"We have only two jobs between now and when school starts. Finding alcohol and meeting guys," said Brees, one of my hometown friends who was also attending Purdue.

There was a longer-term strategy too. For many women, freshman year was when they began hunting for the man of their dreams. Their clocks wouldn't strike midnight until graduation. Most were presumably on the "princess path" with four years of college to land a prince—their ticket to an engagement ring and the good life as a stay-at-home mom.

"The odds are in our favor, Brees," I said. "Do you realize that male students outnumber female students two-to-one at Purdue?"

"You know I hate math, but why do you think I chose this university?" replied Brees. "The guys at our high school were so lame. Let's get this party started!"

Like Brees, I hadn't dated much in high school. At nearly six feet tall, my standards for eligible guys were high, and in more ways than one. College offered a new frontier. I couldn't control the timing of meeting my prince, but I knew he'd eventually find me, as the fairy tale goes. For now, I wanted to do well in school and earn my degree. *That* I knew I could do.

By the time I was a sophomore in college, I'd secured an A average and had become a more socially polished coed.

"Was your summer at home as boring as mine?" a sorority sister asked me as our group entered the massive ivy-covered red brick of the Beta fraternity house, home to sons of doctors and future captains of industry.

"Yes! Worked every minute. So ready for this first kegger of the fall!" I replied.

Once inside, I paused at the balcony and gazed down at the Great Hall, soon to be filled with uninhibited college students drinking and dancing the night away. Then I confidently stepped down the broad, wooden, curved staircase to the main level like a princess arriving at a ball.

Only a few Betas stood along the long wooden bar, but soon the word would be out that the Pi Phi sorority girls were in the house. The Betas had organized a high-volume beverage operation with dozens of filled cups lined up and ready to go. I grabbed a red plastic cup of foam covering a small amount of lukewarm beer. It was Thursday night, time to flip my academic switch to party mode.

"Where are you from?" a tall enough, dark, and reasonably handsome Beta asked me.

"Originally from Columbus, Indiana, but I moved in seventh—"

"I'm from Columbus!" he said with amazement at the chance of meeting someone else from a town of only 30,000.

We compared notes on people we both knew and shared the names of our favorite hometown restaurants. The Bee Gees song "You Should Be Dancing" was blaring—acting as a call to action. Hastily made pairs headed from the barroom to the Great Hall. We'd both had two beers, and he asked me to dance. This was all standard kegger procedure up to this point—that is, until I saw him dance. As soon as we started, I realized he was anything but standard. This casual social interaction suddenly became something you'd see in a bad movie.

He took over much of the dance floor with his long, lanky limbs flailing in all directions, bumping into other dancers. His chicken-wing elbows were dangerous—sharp, like daggers. He even attempted to do the splits, his long legs spread across the dance floor. He sprang up and tried to bump into me with his hips, a move known as "doing the bump." He nearly knocked me down, and I lost one of my clogs in the scuffle—a wardrobe failure and poor shoe choice for dancing. I was a damsel in distress. I was trying to form an escape plan when another Beta came to my rescue.

Even over the loud din of the music, I heard him say some magical words: "Why are you dancing with him when you could be dancing with me?"

I slipped off my remaining shoe and took the hand of my white knight. He immediately seized command, awkwardly spinning me around and then back out. The song was now "Dancing Queen" by ABBA. He had longish, straight brown hair, parted slightly off-center, so thick it hardly moved when he danced. With his aviator glasses, he looked a bit like John Denver. His dark brown eyes were kind, with smile lines in the corners. Everyone seemed to fade away, even the wild dancer. My rescuer made up for a lack of dancing skills with his wonderful sense of humor. He embellished his steps with goofy facial expressions or an occasional "oops" shrug of his shoulders to show that he didn't take himself too seriously. To my surprise, he dipped me, the back of my head touching the floor by the song's end. I pointed one toe, not for show but to hold my balance. He seemed pleased that he didn't drop me. By the time he pulled me up, I felt lightheaded. I wondered if it was the spinning or the dipping, or maybe I was simply under his spell.

I snapped out of it when the wild dancer reappeared. "Hi, Scott. You stole my partner out there," he said. Without waiting for a reply, he then turned to me and asked, "Need another beer?"

"Thanks, Dick," Scott interjected. "You can bring us two beers."

At this point, I realized three things: (1) the wild dancer from Columbus was named Dick—I hadn't even cared to ask before, (2) the Beta who saved me was named Scott, and (3) polite as he was, Scott was an upperclassman because he could order Dick around. I was grateful the rescue would continue beyond one dance. He made me feel safe.

Dick dutifully left, and Scott turned to me. "Why were you talking to him when you could have been talking to me?"

Laurie, another Pi Phi, had noticed Scott and me dancing at the kegger a few days ago. "You should've been at Purdue's open invitation track meet today," she said. "Your boy Scott Miller won the mile. He killed the competition, including my Beta, who held the mile record in high school. For a fat boy, he sure can run." She was referring to Scott with her last remark. He didn't have the emaciated look of your typical cross-country runner, but I would never have described Scott as "fat." It was more like a slight beer belly around the middle.

"Miller set a record. Millertime!" Laurie laughed loudly at her joke. "Did Miller ask you to the Beta hayride yet?" she continued. "I heard he was going to."

"No, first I've heard of it." It was one thing to dance with someone at a kegger, but a date was next-level. Why was I blushing? After hardly dating in high school, I had experienced a year of collegiate dating and was no longer a rookie. What if Laurie was wrong and Scott didn't ask me? Maybe that would be for the best. I wasn't ready for this. I wished she hadn't told me. I reminded myself that I wasn't like the other girls: *You're a late bloomer. You can focus on school for now, and not look for a husband until after college.* This thought settled me.

"Battle, line six. Deb Battle, call on line six." I heard my name called over the sorority house loudspeaker. My parents never called me, and I lived with all my friends. This call could only mean one thing. I ran to the nearest phone booth and pushed the blinking light.

"I heard you were going with me to the hayride this weekend."

I felt weak when I heard his voice, and my back slid down the Pi Phi phone booth wall to the floor.

"I heard the same thing," I responded. From that moment on, my life was never the same.

CHAPTER 2

Royal Coupling

Aurora imagined the man of her dreams would simply appear one day to rescue her. The Tchaikovsky theme song from Sleeping Beauty proves challenging to get out of your head—along with that dreamy notion about love at first sight and becoming a perfect permanent pairing.

We became known as ScottnDeb and were as inseparable as our names. Our backgrounds were uncannily similar—as if we were the same person. Our parents were approximately the same age and had married almost the same day nearly thirty years before. All four parents had been raised as only children, growing up during the Depression. Scott and I both had two older brothers and an older sister, born in that exact order, all about the same age. We were all blonds, aided by strong chlorine from local swimming pools. Our brothers were athletes. Both dads were high-achieving providers—his dad was a doctor and mine was an executive. We had stay-at-home moms who seemed greatly relieved child-rearing had ended. He was even the same height as me. He openly admired my height, along with my metabolism.

"Since I stopped training full-time, beer is taking its toll, not to mention the carbs from nightly pizza," he sighed. "You drink as much beer as any Beta, but you're still a stick. How do you do it?"

Instead of smiling at the compliment, I remembered a slumber party in the seventh grade. Margaret Albright had said, "Battle looks like a stork. How can you even walk on those skinny legs?" All the girls laughed. "And you are pigeon-toed too. Oh my God! We have a rare pigeon-toed stork in our midst!"

"Seriously, though," he went on. "You're pretty perfect. Regal in appearance. You could pass Queen Elizabeth's scrutiny to marry Charles."

I attempted to curtsy. But I wasn't the only one raised to meet royal standards. Scott credited his dad, an anesthesiologist at the Indiana University (IU) Medical Center in Indianapolis, for his good manners. Doctors seemed to run in the family as his sister married an ob-gyn. Scott's face lit up when he talked about his sister, Suzy. He pulled a picture from his wallet to show me her son, the cutest blond toddler ever. Right then, I knew he wanted a family as much as I did.

Scott's smile turned to tears when he told me his dad had been diagnosed with Parkinson's disease a few years ago and now struggled to walk and talk normally. He said nobody at Purdue knew. I'd never seen a boy cry before, even in the movies.

Scott was the loyal type, the ultimate good guy. He would never break anyone's heart or trust—let alone that of someone he loved. He was a keeper.

Relationships take time... especially when you think you've met your prince. I wanted to make space for Scott even though I had precious little spare time. I'd been elected sorority treasurer. It was the only paid officer position because it required accounting skills to calculate payroll and pay taxes for the house operations staff. Dad had made me prepare my taxes since I started working at age sixteen, and I caught on quickly. The money would come in handy as I had to pay for half of my college tuition, which was challenging while earning minimum wage.

The sorority expected its members to participate in campus activities. I was a staff writer for the university newspaper. Seeing my name in print was weird, but I liked it. And I earned a seat on the Grand Prix Junior Board, which added to my résumé.

"Don't Betas do any extracurricular activities?" I asked Scott on a particularly busy day.

"I have my running," he said, sounding satisfied. He had decided not to join the cross-country team because he'd had a bad experience with his previous college coach before transferring to Purdue and preferred to run independently. Scott's laid-back approach to school was new to me. He didn't keep a checkbook or carry around a planner like most students.

"My mom deposits money now and then," he said sheepishly. "I still help cut the grass back home."

In contrast to Scott's unlimited funds, and despite my dad's professional success, my parents only gave me a small stipend at the beginning of each semester. It was enough to buy pizza once a week. Since all the money I earned during the summers went toward tuition, I had no spending money.

Our study habits were also different. Scott struggled as an engineering major and was content to merely pass. He was intelligent but said his dad worked too hard, and he didn't want to be like him. Scott preferred to exert the minimum effort required. In contrast, I always tried to earn an A and generally figured out what it took to accomplish that. Over time, I positively influenced his grades, and he probably lowered my GPA.

"What are you doing right now?" he asked when he called one Sunday afternoon.

"Studying for an econ test."

"Come over to the co-rec fields. Some of us are going to play a pickup game of soccer."

"I really shouldn't."

"You really should. It's seventy degrees and sunny. This may be the last perfect day this fall."

I sighed. "All right." It was easy to play hooky when Scott asked.

I can't recall ever being hugged as a child. I never saw my parents kiss or hold hands. We didn't do that in my family. My sister had distanced herself from me socially for as long as I could remember. My brothers were both a lot older than me and lived in their own worlds. No family members wrote or called me when I went away to school. Scott's mom told him she was "tired of raising children." I'm sure my parents were as well. I always felt like I had pretty much raised myself. With ScottnDeb, I felt loved for the first time in my life.

It was time to take our relationship to the next level. My decision did not come from uncontrolled physical attraction. Scott was particularly good at kissing and cuddling, and I would have been content to stay in that phase for a long time. But I recognized that he was "the one." The one to have children with—and for both of us, that was the ultimate goal in life. Kids. We were already talking about the children we'd have in the future—after marriage. So, now I could take the big risk.

Without consulting anyone, I walked to the health center one day to get birth control pills. And at our next alcohol-infused party at the Beta house, my hands didn't discourage Scott's hands when they roamed. We headed for his room but noticed smoke wafting out the doorway from several stoned Betas and a big bong. But Scott was motivated. He located an empty room around the corner and ushered me to the bed. A short time later, someone opened the door. How could it not have been locked? The bright hallway light stunned the two embarrassed people under the bedcovers. The intruder apologized and closed the door. The heat of shame from wondering if we'd been identified was far worse than any physical pain I suffered that night, although alcohol eased the way. It was not the kind of "special" evening a virgin might have expected.

It wasn't long before Scott officially proposed. He simply asked, "When's the wedding?" While it wasn't the most romantic proposal, asking *when* we would get married was the right question. Scott was two years older than me, but neither of us could imagine separating for even a few days, like over the holidays, let alone waiting for me to graduate. I told him I'd tested out of a few classes and could graduate a year early if I added a couple of summer classes.

"That's great news! It's taking me five years to graduate, and you'll be out in three. But will your parents allow that?" he asked.

"Haven't I told you about my first trip to Purdue? I thought we'd shared everything by now."

Lesson 2—Be Smart, but Not Too Smart

Purdue requires incoming first-year students to visit campus one summer day to meet with their counselor and select classes. When my high school buddies Harper and Brees, our three moms, and I drove to Purdue, our primary goal was to look over our future dorm rooms. We wanted to take measurements and finalize decorating plans for the fall. Upon arrival, the moms left to find coffee and we girls met with our advisors to get the academic business out of the way.

"Deb Battle?" called Randy Shields, student advisor and grad assistant in the School of Management.

"I've reviewed your high school file and your SAT scores," he said as we talked about my fall classes. "It's impressive. We're going to keep you busy here today. I think it will pay off."

"Thanks," I replied unenthusiastically. I didn't like the sound of the "busy" remark as I was supposed to meet my friends as soon as I broke loose from this appointment.

"You'll be taking some tests for the next few hours. Depending on how well you do, you could earn some college credit before you even start school in the fall—chemistry, English, a language," he explained, assuming I would be pleased.

Hours! Taking tests! No, thank you, I thought. But I didn't see that I had any choice. "Okay," I said softly, wondering why I'd invested four years in taking Spanish. We were told it would expand our worldview. Today, my campus view would be a classroom, not a dorm room. *Fine, let's get on with it.* One thing was sure: I would give it my best if I was taking a test. If Randy Shields thought I could test out of some college classes,

I should think so too. Decorating our dorm room would have to wait.

I alerted the girls to my change in plans and spent the next few hours running from one end of campus to another, taking college-level exams in unknown, faraway buildings. Meanwhile, my friends stuck to the original plan and explored the campus and dorm rooms after their brief scheduling appointments. As the moms and daughters drove home later that day, the girls told me everything I'd missed.

"Metal bunk beds. Concrete block walls. The closets don't have any doors over them! Weird. We'll have to hang some beads or something," Harper, my future roommate, called from the third row of Brees's family's large International Travelall vehicle. "I think there's room for both of our stereos if we put one on top of the mini-fridge."

Brees extended her hand from the back row over to my seat. "Let me see your schedule, Battle." I passed it back without looking. My stomach growled, reminding me I'd missed lunch too. "Looks like you've tested out of at least twenty hours, including two years of Spanish!" Brees exclaimed with wide eyes. "Don't let it go to your head or anything, but you're practically a sophomore already."

I was only half listening, my head filled with random Spanish words still spinning around from the test. It had been conducted entirely in Spanish, and I could still feel the large headphones hugging my ears. I kept replaying the questions and rethinking my answers. *Espero haberlo hecho bien—I think I did okay.* Was that right?

Mom leaned over and whispered loudly, "You never even looked at your room! Where are your priorities? The other girls were already meeting some nice boys. And you were off taking tests."

There she goes, I thought, *trying to marry me off*. I wished I could roll my eyes—*mis ojos*. I couldn't stop myself.

She couldn't either, and hissed, "Why do you always hide behind your stupid books? You are so selfish! Why couldn't you be like the other girls for once in your life?"

I didn't think anyone heard Mom, but I didn't want to argue with her in front of them. There was no point in explaining the mandated tests; she would never understand. She believed my life would consist solely of marriage and motherhood. I wanted those things too, especially the motherhood part. That was the plan. I was eighteen and had just completed her training program to understand society's expectations for young women. She'd shown me the traditional path I was supposed to take.

But I turned to the window and stared at the cornfields. *I'm not like the other girls, Mom. Pero no soy como las otras chicas, Mamá.* Academics came easily to me. Purdue seemed to believe in me. I was beginning to think it might be possible for me to have some professional ambitions too. And maybe that could be a good thing for my children. I closed my eyes. I knew I was going places, with or without some nice boy.

No, ScottnDeb wouldn't face any objections from Mom when we eventually shared our good news. And Dad would appreciate one less year of tuition contributions. Randy Shields had been right. I was glad I'd invested my time in taking those tests. Now, I could graduate a year early. *Muy bien.*

CHAPTER 3

Following Tradition

nce Cinderella found her love match, life was good. Everything was going according to plan, er, path.

We agreed not to share our engagement news with anyone until Scott scraped together enough for a ring. He would interview for a job in engineering, and we'd marry and move to wherever that job took us. I would soon officially be on the traditional princess path.

I wasn't nervous about meeting his parents; I viewed it as another job interview. Scott was sure I would *not* like his mom. He coached me to avoid topics like religion, politics, or abortion. I promised to be on my best behavior. Although Scott didn't seem to care about the big picture, like getting a job someday, he was overly concerned with all the little things in life, which probably explained the deep worry lines on his forehead.

"The only thing you need to worry about today is being late because you're driving below the speed limit," I said.

"My father's son," he replied, not budging on the speed. "We'll be even later because I need to stop for gas."

"You have almost half a tank to go another twenty miles!" I said, leaning over to confirm.

"Exactly."

I nodded. "Okay, Grandpa." This wasn't the right moment to tell him about when I'd run out of gas twice in one day on a high school ski trip to Michigan with my friends.

Scott's mom opened the door. "Hello, Scotty. This must be Debra."

"You can call me Deb."

"Let's have a chat in the living room, Debra." Her heels clicked on the hardwood floor, competing with the loud ticking of the grandfather clock.

"It-it-it's nice to meet such a beautiful lady," stuttered Scott's dad, entering from another doorway. He stooped over and shuffled as he slowly approached us. Parkinson's disease was evident in everything except his spirit. "How'd you get a date with her, Scott?" He grinned.

He nearly tripped trying to position a chair for me, and you could tell where Scott had learned to be such a gentleman. Dr. Jerry Miller had a buzz cut and wore thin horn-rimmed glasses, a bow tie, and a wild plaid jacket. His bright blue eyes sparkled.

"Jerry, I'm quite sure she can move her own chair," Peggy interjected, trying to redirect him. His kind expression turned into a frown as he glared at her and continued to arrange my seat before slowly moving to take his own.

Scott jumped in. "He's got it, Mom."

The situation was awkward all around, and the silent periods were deafening. "How is everything at the medical center?" I asked Scott's dad.

Parkinson's dulled the speed of his reactions but not his thoughts. Still, before Dr. Miller could respond, Scott's mom jumped in. "Dr. Miller is the number-two man in the anesthesiology department at the medical center—which is a teaching hospital."

"Well-well-well, my students are working on some promising research at the moment," Dr. Miller said, and began to outline their latest study.

"Debra doesn't care about the research, Jerry."

"No, really, it's—"

"Mom, let him explain," pleaded Scott, but she'd already ruined the moment.

His mom turned to me. "Scott tells us your father is the chief engineer at his organization."

"Yes, he's—"

"And like our Scotty, you have two brothers and a sister. Did you get your height from your father?"

"Well, *both* of my parents are pretty tall . . ."

"I see. And Scott tells me you are a Pi Beta Phi sorority member."

I nodded, and she smiled approvingly. "I was a member of Chi Omega."

Scott mumbled, "For one year before you married Dad."

She ignored him and continued the interrogation, which she completed over a formal lunch in the dining room. I was thankful for the loud clock and the occasional clink of silverware to cover the sounds of my chewing. Etiquette lessons from Mother LeVore, my sorority house mother, came in handy as Peggy's dark brown eyes observed my every move. Toward the end of the torture session, Scott gestured to silently ask whether I minded if he left to cut the grass. I nodded, and he excused himself. After helping to clear the dishes, I excused myself to study.

"If only my children had taken more interest in their studies." Peggy sighed and insisted on a complete house tour before releasing me to study in peace.

I must have aced the interview because Scott said his mom called later to rave about me. Given that she never said anything positive to him, he took that as high praise. One set of parents down, one to go. Even though we weren't ready to tell our parents we were planning to marry, we still wanted these traditional "meet the parents" sessions to go well.

I knew my parents would be easy on Scott. For years, Mom had made it clear that she was desperate for grandchildren. There needed to be a wedding first, which required a mate. While I was the youngest of her four children, there were no serious prospects for the other three. My older sister had never been on a date, and neither brother showed any interest in settling down. Mom was thrilled to meet a suitor as it offered hope that she might become a grandmother someday, like all her friends. The drive to Fort Wayne took hours. It gave Scott time to grow nervous. "What if your dad doesn't like me?"

"You're an engineer like him. It'll be fine."

"I'm a nobody *industrial* engineer; he's *mechanical*. That's a big difference. MEs look down upon IEs. They think we're not really engineers."

"Relax!"

"I don't know. My grades are pretty bad." Scott continued to worry.

"They won't ask about your grades. They just want their daughter married off. On the plus side, you won't have to cut the grass today."

Scott charmed my mom with his outstanding manners, but she'd have welcomed any male I brought home.

"I heard your sister has a little boy—and your brother too! I've waited so long for grandchildren. I just love babies! Let me show you some pictures of Debbie when she was little."

"Mom, it's okay. He doesn't need to see any . . ." *How embarrassing*. But I realized it was hopeless. The good news was that this wouldn't take long—there were only a few photos of me as a child. By the time my parents had their fourth child, they weren't that interested in documenting their children. They'd only taken a few snapshots to mark my entire childhood. But I settled in when she brought out the stack of albums for my oldest brother, Tom. This would take a while. Scott was a trouper and listened to stories of Tom's glory while we flipped through his albums.

"You didn't tell me that Tom was an Eagle Scout who went on to win the Little 500 cycling race at IU, qualify for the Olympics, and captain IU's national championship soccer team," Scott said as we drove back to school.

"Welcome to my childhood," I said.

"I'm marrying up. I hope our children get the Battle height. But why did your mom keep asking if you knew your size?"

I held up my left hand, wiggling my fingers. Mom wanted me to be prepared.

Lesson 3—Know Your Size

"I just love that commercial," Mom said one year when I was in elementary school.

It was one of those De Beers television ads—the romantic kind where the guy proposes to the girl and gives her a giant engagement ring. And they flash up some message like, "Diamonds are forever," or "How else could two months' salary last forever?" I don't think Dad looked up from his newspaper, but that didn't stop Mom from trying.

Before Christmas, she stopped at the jewelry store. She had them check her ring size and update their records since there had been a slight change.

"Just in case he wants to surprise me," she said.

"But I like your ring, Mom," I said.

"It's not bad," Mom replied, looking down at her ring. "They didn't have the best selection right after World War II when he was looking. He did get the right size; I made sure of that."

"I thought you were surprised when he asked you," I said, recalling the family legend.

"I was surprised he was *first*. I'd written my ring size in letters I sent overseas to three boys in the service. Dad wasn't the only one I told."

That was new information. But Mom always told us kids to "be prepared." Now I understand that included knowing (and sharing) my ring size.

After crossing the parental visits off the list, we visited Scott's sister, Suzy, her husband, Jack, and baby Ben for a weekend. Suzy was a wonderful mother and role model. She actively engaged with her toddler, teaching him and positively encouraging him. Like me, Scott and Suzy had grown up in a family that didn't express much love. But now, she was the opposite. Fun and engaging—the kind of mom I always wanted to be.

She'd reached the happily ever after! Suzy's life was a fairy tale—she even lived on a golf course.

That summer, I landed an internship back home at International Harvester (IH), where Dad worked. I took classes at night and studied on the weekends, which didn't leave much time to think about how much my heart ached to be with Scott. He stayed on campus retaking some classes to improve his grades so he could graduate the following year.

Dad and I carpooled. Usually, he dropped me off. On my last day of work for the summer, I asked to keep the car so I could drive to a farewell lunch with my team. At five o'clock, I circled back to pick up Dad. I hadn't driven him since our last driving lesson years before, and it felt weird. He looked mad as he stormed toward the car on the long sidewalk outside his office building. Maybe he thought I'd been driving too fast or stopped too suddenly. Then I noticed he was carrying a cardboard box, which he threw into the back seat, and slammed the door. Sitting next to me, he looked like a volcano about to erupt. Dad had never been mad at me before; that was Mom's department. I assumed he'd want to drive, but he just sat in the passenger seat and stared straight ahead. I guessed he was letting me drive home, so I pulled out, signaled right, and went as slowly and carefully as possible.

We drove in silence for a few miles. He was sweating profusely, just staring. He never once looked at me. Maybe it wasn't my driving. I finally said, "Is everything okay?"

Dad was a just-the-facts kind of guy. But he struggled to find the words to answer me, his youngest daughter. "My position was eliminated today," he said, still staring blankly ahead, like a zombie.

Forget the Fairy Tale and Find Your Happiness

No! Dads didn't lose jobs. Not my dad, anyway. Dads traditionally take care of their families. How could this be? Did Mom know? How would he find another job when he was fifty-four years old?

I didn't know what to say. "Was this a surprise?" was all I could manage.

There was a long pause before he spoke. "I saw some smoke, but not the fire," he finally answered, staring out the window, unable to meet my eyes.

I didn't know what to say to a man who had lost his livelihood. He'd always received promotions and industry accolades, never a pink slip. We drove in silence the rest of the way. At least I'd have some good news for him this weekend when Scott arrived. He'd officially ask for my hand, and we'd announce our engagement before returning for the fall semester. My fairy tale was about to begin.

Back at campus, I wanted to conceal our big news from the Pi Phis for a few hours. I was nervous about losing my ring, so I fastened it to the elastic waistband inside my gym shorts with a safety pin. It was comforting to feel it resting on my stomach at dinner that evening. Mother LeVore tapped her water glass, and the room quieted. "Ladies, we will be having a pinning circle ceremony tonight." The room buzzed with anticipation. *Who could it be?* the girls wondered. After a long summer, a few engagements would be expected. My name never came up during the usual speculation at dinner about who might be the lucky girl. Most girls considered me a junior, too young to be engaged.

Traditionally, "pinning circles" signaled that a girl had received a fraternity lavalier, pin, or engagement ring. I'd witnessed many ceremonies with eighty girls in the house; someone was always locking down their man. Hardly anyone was lavaliered these days; the couples went straight to pin or ring. The sorority president would light a candle and start passing it from girl to girl around a circle. If the candle was blown out in the first round, it signified that the girl who blew it out had received a lavalier from a fraternity boy. The second round meant a pin, and waiting until the third round meant an engagement announcement. The song was brief, and you'd think the repetition would drive you crazy, but we never seemed tired of being part of each girl's special moment.

As we locked arms and started singing that night, I looked at each face in the glow of the candle as it moved around the circle. Everyone was looking for some sign to identify the lucky girl. The pinning song passed two rounds, and the girls knew someone was engaged. The singing voices grew louder as their anticipation heightened.

My heart was throbbing. I never wanted to be the center of attention. I hadn't confided in anyone because I wanted to surprise the girls. I was second-guessing my decision to keep a secret this big to myself. The muscles around my knees began to spasm. Thank God we'd all linked arms, which provided security that I wouldn't collapse if my legs gave out. The three rounds seemed to take forever. When the candle got to me on the third round, I barely mustered enough strength to blow it out.

My news was completely unexpected; no one had ever graduated early. On the surface, everyone seemed happy for

Scott and me, though some girls may have experienced a feeling of panic with only a limited time left in college to complete their MRS degree.

Later, my friend, Smitty expressed a different take. She got right to the point when I outlined our plans to marry next summer. "How can you even think about throwing away your future?"

"What do you mean?" was all I could say, wondering if it was a jealous reaction.

"Don't get me wrong. Scott is a nice guy and all. But you're *different*," Smitty said.

I was tired of being "different," the girl who was too tall, too thin, or too smart. I never wanted to be different.

Her tone softened when she saw my tormented face. "You're only twenty."

"I'll be twenty-one. My mom was only nineteen, and it worked out for her."

"I thought our generation was starting to move past this whole 'marriage and follow *his* career' idea. In your case, if it's true love, he should follow *you. You* could get a great job and go places," Smitty suggested. "Scott—nicest guy ever, but he spends his time going on and off academic probation, from what I can see."

True, I thought, gazing out the second-story sorority house window facing the main campus street. As a sorority officer, I'd earned a room with a view. I cranked open the window and a warm gust of air filled the room. In the evening light, I could see the sidewalks swarming with the arriving students—each with a dream. I pictured myself at a fork, faced with two life path choices: having a family *or* having a career. There used to be only one path, but feminism had opened another. I firmly believed that women should be able to pursue any career—if they wanted one. But I'd never seen a woman who had both. I'd found Scott early in life, so I didn't need a job. That dream had faded away. Taped on the wall was one of my inspirational posters: *Without dreams, life is a broken-winged bird that cannot fly.*

"Don't you see?" I murmured, still looking out the window. "I'll be living the dream."

"Whose dream?" she demanded. "Battle, wake up! That was society's dream for women—to control our bodies. But the rules are changing. We've got the ERA, Roe v. Wade. And 1977 is International Women's Year. With your brain, you could go anywhere!"

Just then, a large gust of wind slammed the door shut.

"Maybe that will snap you out of it," Smitty continued, unfazed. "I thought you were a feminist."

She had a point. On the one hand, I considered myself a feminist. I'd secretly arranged for Scott and I to drive a good friend of mine hours away to the only available abortion clinic the week before. But on the other hand, I'd grown up with only stay-at-home moms as role models. With Scott, I had my first chance to take that traditional princess path. I looked at the ring on my left finger, a sparkling emerald cut, set at a diagonal—pointing up, precisely as I'd designed it for the jeweler. I'd trained my whole life for this moment. I'd found my prince, we loved each other, and we'd ride to our happily ever after. *That's the path a girl is supposed to be on, right?* I asked myself, my eyes returning to the window. The curtains danced in the breeze, framing the campus, a world of dreams.

Forget the Fairy Tale and Find Your Happiness

"Whatever happened to grad school in California?"

"That was before..."

"Before what? You lost your mind?"

"Before Scott. I never thought I'd meet the right guy, or *any* guy, so soon. I thought I had time."

"You have time; you have your whole life. You think you love him, but he's only your first boyfriend. How can you know for sure?" Smitty tried one last time to reach me. "Why would you throw away all your hard work studying when you're almost there?" She turned and left.

I stretched out on the daybed. Graduate school and a career had always been my backup plan if the princess path didn't work out. But I *had* to have kids. Choosing a job over kids wasn't an option. Suddenly, I missed Scott. He'd make me feel better. I thought, *I should call him and let him know how it went with the pinning circle.* But what would I say to him about *this* conversation? The warm breeze made me sleepy.

Smitty was talking nonsense. I couldn't throw away my chance at having a family. She'd implied that I shouldn't be the girl at the center of a pinning circle on my way to a life in the suburbs, just like my high school peers had thought when they voted me least likely to marry before age thirty. I took it as a slam back then because I'd not dated much, but maybe there was more to it. I closed my eyes. Was something different about me? Marriage was the traditional path to happiness. Wasn't that what we girls had been raised to do?

SECTION II

Living the Dream

Cinderella dreamed that she and her prince would live happily ever after. But how do we know that's what happened? Why does Cinderella's story end right when she marries the guy?

CHAPTER 4

Once Upon a Time

It would be tough to top a kiss like that—from a prince that sets you free after a hundred years. No wonder Aurora waltzed straight to the altar and married that guy, even if she was only sixteen.

It wasn't true love's kiss that awakened me on the morning of our wedding. It was the strong smell of Lysol in Teresa's Indianapolis apartment. From my horizontal view, I could see her disinfecting the bathroom counters, which I must have sullied somehow. Even the pillowcase where my head lay smelled antiseptic. I couldn't complain; Teresa insisted I sleep in her bed since I was getting married, and she took the couch. It was strange but nice to see her on her own, out from under Mom and Dad's shadow, where she'd been ever since a long childhood illness. Perhaps her comfort with sterile environments led to her profession as a nurse.

I couldn't get the refrain to "Chapel of Love" out of my head as we drove to the church in Teresa's little yellow Pinto. I was getting married! I wasn't nervous, but maybe I should've been. I was only twenty-one years old. What was I doing? I remembered how rough it had been last summer without Scott every day. Daily letters and weekly long-distance calls weren't enough to sustain our aching hearts. Getting married was the right thing to do, especially after Dad lost his job. My parents were moving soon. ScottnDeb. He was my home now.

Dad and I stood in an alcove at the rear of the church. He rehearsed his one line in his deep voice: "Her *mother* and I do. Her mother and *I* do. Her mother and I *do*." If it were up to me, we could skip this tradition of a father handing off his daughter like she's some piece of property. He glanced at his watch. I figured he was calculating whether he had enough time to duck out and have a cigarette.

Standing at the sanctuary door, Mom must've figured the same; she disapprovingly shook her head at him and signaled that she was ready to begin her long walk down the aisle to the front row. She looked regal on my eldest brother Tom's arm as the mother of the bride. Even Queen Elizabeth couldn't match Mom's elegant posture, her head held high on that invisible string she often talked about. Mom frequently compared herself to the queen because they shared the same birth year and had four children. When Princess Anne married a few years ago, Mom encouraged Tom to keep pace. Today, Mom proudly evened the score with Her Majesty. Now, they'd share the wait to produce heirs. Hosting a wedding had to be one of the social highlights of her life, and it appeared she enjoyed every moment of the attention. Mom had given me a lot of guidelines about society's expectations, but the only advice she offered for my marriage was to put body lotion on my elbows nightly for a few months leading up to the ceremony. By softening them up, I could avoid wrinkled elbows as I walked down the aisle on my wedding day. Oops. That didn't happen. I had wrinkled elbows for my wedding. But I did straighten my posture—just for you, Mom.

The wedding procession continued with five bridesmaids in peach-colored formals on the arms of groomsmen in tan tuxedos. The organist played a fanfare to cue us in the back. I tried to step forward as rehearsed, my arms interlocked with Dad's, but he was frozen. He said aloud, as if advising himself, "Take three deep breaths and put one foot in front of the other."

I never once doubted the love Scott and I had for each other, and I couldn't wait another minute to begin our happily ever after. Perhaps it was Dad's nervousness, or maybe because I was already a natural businessperson constantly weighing alternatives, but the last thing I thought as Dad and I took our first steps was, *If it doesn't work out, there's always the divorce option.*

The reception was a fairy tale. Champagne flowed as guests mingled around the historic Lilly estate on the Indianapolis Museum of Art grounds. They posed in and around the fountains, imitating the sculptures, even Robert Indiana's idyllic *LOVE* sculpture. Think Y-M-C-A. Other friends stayed inside and did their best imitations of John Travolta on the dance floor while the DJ played hits from *Saturday Night Fever*. Mom was spotted jitterbugging to the '70s music on the tiny dance floor with whoever would join her.

As happy as she was to host a wedding, Mom couldn't resist registering a few complaints. "I don't know why you insisted upon birdseed packets at the church for the send-off. I can't get that seed out of my hair!"

"It's okay to break tradition—seed is better for the birds than rice," I tried to explain.

"What if birds attack me? Look, those boys are taking whole bottles of champagne and heading to the gardens!"

"Mom, stop. Please. They brought those bottles themselves. See the label? Please don't make trouble."

Later, there was cause for her concern. She was on the terrace, near the fountain, talking to a lifelong friend. Lea had produced four sons but initially no daughter, so Mom named me after her—for my middle name. Lea pulled Mom aside for a chat to share some news. "Walt asked for a divorce." Walt and Lea attended the wedding together and chose to use the occasion as a platform for communicating their news. Now, my parents' special day was tainted by bad news.

Dad used to joke, "When Mom hits age forty, I'm going to trade her in for two twenties."

Well, Walt had found himself a younger woman—only one, but he *was* leaving his wife. Mom wondered what was to become of Lea. Even with some alimony, she would have to enter the job market for the first time at age fifty-two without a college education. Her prince had left her. Lea was alone—forced off the path. "I'll probably never see her again," Mom predicted.

Nicknamed our Moneyhoon, Scott had been able to siphon (barely) enough money from his college checking account for us to spend five days on Paradise Island by Nassau. He didn't feel comfortable asking his parents for money, so Scott regularly wrote checks for cash and set the money aside.

"Just ask them. I don't think they'd mind chipping in for their son's honeymoon," I said.

But Scott didn't like to discuss matters of money. Without consulting his parents, this was Scott's way of fulfilling the tradition for the groom to fund the honeymoon. The budget was tight, but we headed to Paradise, the perfect place to start our new life together. We flew economy class and stayed at a Holiday Inn. We economized on meals by sharing a breakfast and eating fast food for dinner. There was just enough left to split one entrée at a sit-down restaurant on our last night. Our tight budget allowed about ten dollars for one shot at entertainment. Jet Skis, boat rides, or fishing trips were out of the question, but we *could* afford to rent a motorbike. After convincing Scott it would be safe, we rode together one glorious day on the oceanside drive that circled the island of New Providence.

"I think we need to retire in Florida someday!" I shouted in his ear as we rode, enjoying the warm, salty air. I loved the tropical climate and couldn't get enough sunshine. I spent every waking moment outside trying to get a tan while listening to the sound of the waves.

"Too hot and humid there!" he called back. "But I *am* looking forward to retiring. My forty-plus-year jail sentence starts next week."

"That's depressing. How can you think like that? Just imagine—by our second anniversary, with both of us working, we'll have saved enough for a down payment on a real house!" After that, we'd be ready to start our family.

"Great. Then I can celebrate being married to a mortgage."

Forget the Fairy Tale and Find Your Happiness

Long walks on the soft, white, sandy beach didn't cost anything. The filming location for *Thunderball*, a recent James Bond movie, was a short hike away, and we snorkeled in a coral-protected bay at our hotel. Paddling around on the surface of the crystal-clear water, we watched schools of bright blue and yellow fish dart around the slowly waving plants and pink coral anchored in the white sand. At one point, Scott was sure he saw a barracuda and wildly signaled for me to join him as he paddled back to shore. I decided to take my chances. When I finally swam back, I found Scott sitting on the striped hotel towel. Deeper furrows than usual lined his forehead. "You're not afraid of anything, are you?" he asked in his sternest voice.

"I'm afraid of sunburn," I said, smiling, reaching for the lotion to reapply.

"No, Deb, I saw a barracuda. It was dangerous to stay out there."

Was he trying to scold me, or was that embarrassment I detected in his voice? I'm pretty sure there was no barracuda, but I decided not to challenge his masculinity on our honeymoon.

"I'm afraid of missing out on something," I said. "Fun. Beauty. Life. When will I get another chance to snorkel in the turquoise waters of the Caribbean? I'm a girl—the fourth child. We have to make our own opportunities. When you see a chance, you take it."

CHAPTER 5

Time Flies

*S*ure, Snow White faced obstacles along the way to her happily ever after, such as being temporarily banished deep into the forest. She kept it positive even while cleaning up after seven male strangers. But did the emphasis on Snow's handy housework skills reinforce the stereotype that a woman's place is in the home?

I picked at my skin, peeling it off in the spots most damaged by the tropical sun during our glorious honeymoon. My sunburned legs stuck to the U-Haul's hot vinyl seats, and each stop proved painful as I extracted myself. We drove across Indiana to collect used furniture from our parents' basements for our new life together. Last, we picked up the two kittens we'd selected a few weeks ago. ScottnDeb had a family. Now, we just needed to save up a bit before we could begin my life's work as a mom.

Engineers were in high demand. Even with a C average, Scott received a job offer from NCR in Dayton, Ohio, upon graduating from Purdue. I got a job there too. We'd been on one house-hunting trip earlier that month and discovered a new condominium complex called The Habitat. As a business student, I'd calculated that with an initial deposit of $1,500, our monthly payments would be like rent, and we could sell the condo later for a profit. After paying the last of my tuition, I had precisely that amount left in my savings account, earned from my internship last summer. So, we decided to buy a condo even before the wedding. My sunburn had become a golden tan by the time we pulled up to our new home, and Scott carried me over the threshold. Living the dream.

If only Dayton weren't hilly. The stick shift on Scott's black Mercury Comet terrified me. On my first attempt, I nearly rolled back into another car at a stoplight on a hill. I handed back his keys, and Scott did all the driving. We worked on the same campus, and he dropped me off and picked me up at the corporate finance building. My boss told me my employment was an experiment—I was the first female in the department *and* the first employee in the department without an MBA. If I failed, I wasn't sure which demographic would take the blame, but I did feel a strong sense of responsibility to succeed—even if I only planned to work until I got pregnant.

"Let's both get master's degrees!" I said to Scott on the way home one day. "We can go at night." I was supercompetitive, and if the guys at work all had MBAs, I wanted one too. I didn't need another degree to be a mom, but I could earn more if I had those three letters after my name—maybe not as much as the guys in my department, but the company would pay more than my current salary. It was a once-in-a-lifetime "free" (company-paid) opportunity. So, there was no doubt in my mind about going for it.

Scott looked at me as if I were crazy. "You seriously want to go back to school? Right after we got out?"

"The guys at work say it's a lot easier to go back right *after* undergrad . . . before you lose the school habit. They say after you have kids, there's no time."

"After *you* have kids, *you'll* have all the time in the world—because you won't be working."

"I don't think Suzy would say she has a spare minute to work on a degree," I said, reminding him of how busy his sister, the mother of two young children, was. "And besides, if we do it now, the company will pay for it. And someday, I'll probably return to work—if I'm good at it."

"You are great at everything. But what would *I* do with an MBA?"

"You don't have to get *an* MBA. An MS helps engineers move up—into management."

"I don't think I'll ever be a manager. And it took me five years to finish the last degree going full-time. I can't imagine how long it would take to complete one going at night." Scott sighed his heaviest sigh.

"The guys said we'd finish in less than two years. I'll get an MBA; you can get an MS in management science. I already checked out the requirements for acceptance."

"The plan is for you to quit after two years. Why spend all your time now working and going to school every night?"

I waved a brochure at him as he drove. "I'll be a well-educated mom! I walked over at noon today and picked up a course schedule." The University of Dayton (UD) campus was next to the NCR campus. "We only have one car, so we *have* to go together. Two nights a week. These can be your mandatory rest days from running. Come on. You can do this! It'll be good for your future, for our *family's* future!"

"I can already see my future as an engineer. And it's depressing. A life of working in a salt mine every day for forty years," he said. "Maybe my poor grades will save me and they'll reject my application."

I couldn't imagine why a husband or dad would skip any opportunity to move ahead or take better financial care of his family. That was unfathomable to me. I thought dads wanted what was best for their families and were willing to fight for it. But that's not how I convinced him to join me. He reluctantly proceeded because we carpooled.

Two years later, with degrees in hand, Scott and I relocated to Indianapolis and bought a home. We were ready to start our family, and being based in Indiana would make it easier for our kids to see their grandparents. However, the timing was terrible. We couldn't have picked a worse time to transition back home. America was experiencing a real estate crisis. It was the early '80s and mortgage rates hovered near 20 percent when we bought our first house. It was a castle to us.

Across the pond, Lady Diana was about to become an actual princess. The world, including me, watched her storybook wedding as she began her path to a happily ever after. It wasn't long before she was pregnant like everyone else. Years later, Diana famously shared, "Being a princess isn't all it's cracked up to be."

It was a tough job market during these times of super-high inflation, but once again, we found jobs at the same organization. We liked carpooling together even though Scott wanted to leave work each day when the clock struck 4:00 p.m. so he could go running. I'd pack up my papers and continue to work from home. This time, we worked at the Naval Avionics Center (NAC), a large government research and development facility that was part of the Defense Department. I didn't care where I worked. It was just a paycheck until my real work began—raising a family.

But I couldn't help myself. I had to give 100 percent if I accepted an assignment. Once again, I found myself on the fast track with several quick promotions while Scott was on a different track, pouring his energy into competitive running. He ran several marathons, including the prestigious Boston Marathon. At work, he was recognized as a runner, and many sought his advice to develop training plans.

"You hate engineering. Why don't you become a high school teacher and cross-country coach?" I asked.

"Good concept, but there's no way I'd ever go back to school."

I couldn't understand how someone could decide to spend time on work that made them so unhappy. At least Scott enjoyed counting the days until retirement.

Working for the Defense Department during the Reagan presidency was like being in a growth industry. Reagan wanted to strengthen the military, but he also wanted to eliminate or sub out as many non-core function government jobs as possible, such as janitorial or lawn care. I think he wanted to report how many federal jobs he'd cut. I figured out how to cut costs for services *and* save hundreds of jobs for our organization, known as "billets," that could be used for engineering positions in the future. It was a cost accounting exercise, and

I discovered a winning formula. The Naval Air Systems Command in DC noticed our success and solicited me to consult Navy-wide. It would've been a great job if my direct supervisor in Indianapolis hadn't been a jerk.

"You need to fire Floyd," he said one day, peering at me through his black horn-rimmed glasses. His eyewear combined with his beak-like nose and black mustache reminded me of Groucho Marx. But he was no comedian.

"Can I ask why?"

He fumbled with some papers and mumbled, "Don't need any reason. We all know he doesn't belong in our group."

What *I* knew was that I had recently rated him one of the top performers in the department when filling out annual review paperwork for my boss.

"So, it doesn't matter that he's in the top ten percent?" I asked.

"Nope. We already hit the numbers with all the females in the group—including you."

I was still boiling when I told Scott about it on the drive home. "He was implying he didn't need to check a minority box too."

"Floyd is the Black guy you introduced at the company picnic, right?"

"Uh-huh. The one with the pregnant wife," I said.

"Nice guy," Scott said.

"Groucho doesn't fear any pushback from the Affirmative Action Law of 1965. He said there are laws, and then there's what's *done*."

"What did *you* do?" he asked.

"I marched right down to Supply Chain and found Floyd another job."

"Tell me you didn't do that. We can't afford for you to lose your paycheck quite yet."

"He left me no choice! I had to do something. I mean, companies like Cummins in my hometown are pulling out of South Africa over apartheid. It was the least I could do." I knew my boss was a racist. But sometimes Scott forgot that I had been raised differently.

Columbus, Indiana, wasn't just any small town. Lady Bird Johnson nicknamed this oasis for architecture "Athens of the Prairie." The works of world-renowned architects like Eero Saarinen, I.M. Pei, and Harry Weese loomed large and attracted visitors from around the world. The foundation of local corporate royalty, J.I. Miller, paid their architectural fees to design public buildings ranging from schools and post offices to fire stations and even the city jail. But Miller's true gift to the city was that he practiced diversity. Long after slavery had ended but before many workplaces in America began to be inclusive, Mr. Miller set a positive example. He brought foreign nationals and their families to the States for corporate assignments. I thought everyone had neighbors from the UK, Europe, and South America. He even selected a few Black men for leadership positions at his company, Cummins Engine Company, where my dad worked until I was thirteen. Miller also co-sponsored Dr. Martin Luther King's historic 1963 March on Washington, where King outlined his vision for America:

"I have a dream . . ." I grew up thinking this type of support for civil liberties was normal. When I joined the workplace, I learned it was not.

I kept my job, and my boss saw it as a win for him to get Floyd out of his group. And Floyd had a new job in a better place. Floyd's pregnant wife thanked me for taking the risk to go around my boss on behalf of her husband.

The timeline for starting our family kept extending outward. After a while, it seemed like everyone was pregnant but me. I attended baby shower after baby shower. Friends and neighbors all seemed to be having children, but regretfully, we could not. At first, we held off to raise money for a house. Then, it was my biggest fear: infertility. Trying to conceive was wearing us down. Each month felt like a year. Every time my period began, it got tougher to stay positive. I always thought that if you worked hard at something, you would reach your goal, and we'd worked hard at this!

Having children was my top priority in life. ScottnDeb would figure this out. We had to. Eventually, we confided in Scott's sister, Suzy, and her husband, Jack, an ob-gyn. Jack suggested I schedule a visit with his senior partner, Dr. Mackey, at the Indianapolis Medical Center. We thought there could be some infertility issues from Scott's running, but tests ruled that out, indicating the problem was on my side. Jack suggested it wasn't uncommon for women to have difficulty becoming pregnant after being on "those darn little blue pills." He felt the dosage had been too strong for many young women in the early years. He also mentioned that thin women often face difficulties becoming pregnant. That was me: skinny and barren.

When I met with Dr. Mackey, he pointed out the obvious—which had not been obvious to me—that my period cycle was only about three weeks in length versus the usual twenty-eight days. I knew I was cursed! After a few months and some testing, Dr. Mackey's team determined that I had a short luteal phase, about half the length it should have been. The luteal stage comes after ovulation. Mine was only a week, and I was shedding the uterus lining before an egg could take hold. It all seemed unfair. Billions of women got pregnant—why couldn't I? This situation terrified me. I had planned to be a mom all my life—but what if I couldn't? Desperate times called for desperate measures.

"How far do I have to run today?" I asked Scott. For seven years, I'd successfully avoided participating in his hobby. But now I needed to do something that hurt to take my mind off my infertility.

"Well, you should probably do a longer one so you'll be ready for the race next week," he said excitedly, thrilled to have a new student.

"You hit a PR yesterday!" he added, pointing to the running calendar he'd prepared for me.

"Do we need to keep track?" I said, lacing up the Señorita Cortez Nikes he'd bought for me long ago, hoping I'd join him in his life's passion.

"Track! That reminds me. We need to get you to the high school track to do some sprints. It will help develop your kick to finish a race."

"Is that really necessary? And where is this runner's high you keep promising me I'll experience?"

The only thing I dreaded more than these running sessions was our "lovemaking" during the infertility phase of my life. Sex had never been a big part of our relationship, other than as necessary for reproduction. I'd never experienced the kind of orgasm you read about. It was okay with me; I didn't feel I was missing anything. Scott and I were perfect companions. We greatly enjoyed each other's company and shared many interests, even if running was now on the list.

Any romantic passion had been sparked by alcohol over the years until we activated the baby-making plan. From then on, sex became just another unpleasant step in the whole infertility sausage-making process. But finally, after years of limbo, we got pregnant! The infertility drugs must've finally kicked in. It felt like my life could now move forward on the right path. The second-best news? I got to stop running.

"Have you told Groucho you're pregnant yet? He'll die when he hears he's lost his star performer," Scott said.

After working for the past six years, it was time to plan for *not* working. "You know, I'm not sure quitting is going to be the right decision after all," I found myself saying.

"Like I said, you're a star. More and more women are starting to stay in the workforce," he said with a show of support.

Scott was right. Society was beginning to recognize that there was value in two-paycheck families. On television, June Cleaver had been replaced by working mother Clair Huxtable. Scott seemed to have already hit his ceiling and showed no interest in taking steps to advance his career. Ambition was not in his DNA. On his stagnant salary, how could we afford a home in a nice neighborhood with good schools for our kids, like we'd both had growing up? I worried about our family's financial future. Our happily ever after was in doubt.

"I read that, but nobody around here goes back to work," I said. Our neighborhood had no role models; no mom continued to work. None. These women were privileged and stayed home on that traditional princess path, just like mothers had during my childhood. Once they had their babies, their men took care of them.

It pained me, but I knew I could no longer count on Scott. Our kids were sure to have crooked teeth. How could we afford braces? Who would pay for their college educations if Scott's income couldn't? It would probably be up to me if I wanted a specific life for my kids—well-educated children with straight teeth living in a nice house. Should I stay in the workforce or at home? It was an either-or decision. In the early '80s, I could not see any middle ground, no other options. This was the most significant and challenging decision I had ever faced. Sometimes life, or death, has a funny way of answering those big questions for you.

Partway through my pregnancy, Mom called. "Your dad has kidney cancer. They're doing surgery right away."

You never imagine your strong dad could be ill. Dad was only sixty but took this news as a wake-up call and stopped smoking.

"They think they got it all," Mom said after the doctors removed one kidney. But a few months later, as my stomach grew with the baby, Dad's cancer returned.

"They're going to treat him with radiation," Mom told me. "They said he probably will only have five years left."

Crushed that my child would only have a granddad for a short time, I also had questions to ask before it was too late. Dad was my hero—tall, dark, and distinguished—in an Abraham Lincoln sort of way. He had angular features and a five-o'clock shadow; you couldn't miss his oversized ears and thinning hair. Dad was also my professional role model, working long hours on the job. Whip-smart. A recognized leader, he was an innovative visionary. He typically impressed his bosses and advanced up the corporate ladder. Yet I think he did it all to care for his family. I never noticed any ego involved. That's just what dads did. He'd been a good provider. It was strange to see him in a hospital bed now. His suitcase sat in the corner. I remembered how exciting it had been whenever Dad returned from overseas business trips and opened that suitcase laden with gifts from foreign lands. These treasures signaled a world outside of Indiana that I wanted my kids and me to see.

Unlike Mom, Dad only gave advice if asked. Our remaining time together was flying by, so it was time to pose my big question. My brother Tom had always been our family's golden boy, and we all knew it. I was the youngest of four children—the ignored one. But I was the only one to follow Dad into the corporate world, and the only one who was married. With his only grandchild on the way, I needed to know his thoughts on my return to the workplace after the birth. Would it be the best decision to have someone else "raise" my child if I were a provider? Dad understood how much it costs to raise children and the effort it took to be a star at work. He also knew what I thought about my boss, Groucho. "I hate that guy," I reminded him.

Dad's response surprised me. "You don't hate your boss. You've lost respect for him. He's let you down as a manager. Life is too short to give your time to something or someone you don't respect. If you do, you will lose your own self-respect," he said. "If you are asking for my advice, quit work; enjoy that child. A job will always be there for you. If you're good, you'll be good at anything, anytime." He paused. "And you're good."

That was the second time he'd said something like that to me.

Lesson 4—R.E.S.P.E.C.T.

Dad was a man of few words and rarely complimented anyone except my brother Tom. Therefore, his conversation with my high school Spanish teacher at graduation was surprising.

"When the class traveled to Mexico, your daughter saw the poverty and asked many questions. And she always wants to know about my life in Cuba," Señora Rodriguez said to him in her heavy accent.

I smiled, remembering how she'd made me speak to her only in Spanish.

"I respect Deb. She can accomplish anything she wants to," my dad responded.

I was shocked. I had never received a single compliment from my dad—ever. Not when I brought home perfect papers, test scores, or report cards. He was the one person I looked up to, and he respected *me*? I was barely able to sleep that night. I couldn't stop thinking about how my dad believed in me. College was right around the corner. Perhaps my happily ever after could include more than finding a prince and raising a couple of successful kids.

Dad's advice for me to quit came just before he stopped the radiation.

"Dad's back in the hospital with all kinds of tubes to keep him going," Mom said.

That phase didn't last long either. Dad decided to go home and die in his own bed. That's when the morphine started and the food and water stopped.

All four kids made it to Dad's bedside for his final day. The last time I sat alone with him, he was too weak to speak.

"Dad, we're having a girl," I said. I didn't know; there'd been no ultrasound, but I had a strong feeling and wanted him to know about his first grandchild. "We'll call her Hadley Elayne, her middle name after your mom, Mama Dell."

He couldn't open his eyes, but he lightly squeezed my hand. He understood. We played Frank Sinatra's "My Way" at his funeral, and the minister read a poem I'd written about Dad. My pregnant stomach locked up for most of the funeral—the baby felt like a huge, hard ball of tightened muscles. She and I survived the experience together.

Dad worked up until his death in January of 1984. He never got to enjoy retirement or travel for pleasure. His illness and advice helped me to define my path. I decided *not* to return to my full-time job. I'd take the traditional princess path like my mother before me. My mission was to care for and teach that baby; no one could do it like I could. Mom wanted no part of babysitting regularly, and frankly, I wanted a different parenting style for my kids. They would become my life's work. I knew I'd need to work part-time somehow. We needed the money, and it would help me keep one foot in the workplace. I figured there would be plenty of time to fit that in. Maybe I'd even take up golf. After all, how time-consuming could it be to take care of one little princess?

CHAPTER 6

My Royal Family

Ariel, the youngest daughter of King Triton, didn't have to marry to become a royal, but she did sacrifice a promising career as a mermaid to follow a man. She had to morph into a human and almost lost her voice permanently to join his world. Ariel is the only princess that Disney follows into marriage and motherhood, albeit in a sequel. Does the general lack of follow-up mean that a princess's life is no longer interesting after she finds her prince? If so, why? That's when her happily ever after is supposed to begin, not end.

My due date arrived, but not the baby. As difficult as it had been to become pregnant, it seemed almost as difficult to dislodge once the seed was planted. This baby didn't want to leave the womb. I'd agreed to give up my body for nine months, but the thought of going longer than that didn't seem fair—a breach of contract. Mentally, each extra day felt like a week.

My kindly old OB ordered a "stress test" a week after the due date. Ironically, this test was *not* named for the mother's stress after nine months of pregnancy and dealing with an OB unwilling to offer her an inducement date. *This* stress test was to test the placenta's ongoing viability.

After the test, Scott was pleased. "You passed!" It seemed he viewed the healthy placenta "score" as akin to the early academic success of his unborn child. My placenta passing the stress test was no cause for celebration, though. Yes, I was relieved to hear the baby was healthy. But I already knew that firsthand from the constant kicking and rolling. We headed home empty-handed, except for the trusty "just in case" suitcase that had been packed for weeks. Would this baby ever decide to come? The wait continued, with nothing to do but tend to my hemorrhoids and conduct research on the longest time a human baby had ever spent in utero.

Fourteen uncomfortable days past the due date, we held that big bundle of joy. Hadley clocked in at eight pounds, fifteen ounces—that's what you get when your doctor lets you go two weeks late. My labor to deliver her took twenty-two hours, but here's the silver lining: I enjoyed a perfectly timed epidural. Once administered, I did not experience pain; it was like tightening my fist and feeling the pressure, but no pain. *Why is this called "labor"?* I wondered.

"I'll be back tomorrow after work," Scott said, leaving me at the hospital.

"Mom will visit first thing. She'll be so excited to get your call tonight with the news," I said.

"I think all the parents will be surprised it's a girl," Scott said.

Everyone had assumed we'd have a boy. After all, Scott came from a family of three boys; his older siblings had already delivered three male cousins, and my parents had started with two boys. I'm also pretty sure that most people preferred male heirs at the time. Society dictated that boys were entitled to the family name, to participate in sports, to have long and successful careers, *and* to have a family—many things that traditionally had been out of reach for girls, including me. Both grandmothers confirmed their disappointment with their reactions: "You can have a boy next time."

Lesson 5—Titles Matter

Titles bestowed on peers loyal to the Crown have been around for centuries. The titles of duke, marquess, earl, viscount, and baron are hereditary, passed down from generation to generation, but only for males. Title IX was introduced by Senator Birch Bayh from my home state of Indiana when I was partway through high school in 1972. Not every woman was happy about the implications of Title IX and changing women's societal roles.

Mom said, "The only title a woman needs is 'Mrs.'" She worried Bayh's efforts would "cause women to pump their own gas or be drafted to war." No, Mom was not a fan of Senator Bayh, who also authored the Twenty-Fifth and Twenty-Sixth Amendments and was a major proponent of the ERA.

Teachers chose me to represent my high school at Indiana Girls' State in 1974. Mrs. Bayh, a former participant, hosted the prestigious event for top government and history students. She was the first woman I ever saw deliver a speech. Marvella Bayh was a timely role model for me as I had to speak to all five hundred girls and was scared to death. She was majestic—like *she* was a senator. Marvella had it all: beauty and intelligence.

I vowed to vote for any husband (or son) of hers—once I was old enough. My takeaway from her speech was an explanation of Title IX. It was aimed at equal citizenship—education and opportunities for women. Until then, I'd thought it was only about sports.

After Title IX was instituted, my high school added volleyball for girls. It was my chance to play organized sports, but I had never played volleyball. Girls who took advantage of this athletic opportunity became state finalists even if they had to wear boys' basketball junior varsity uniforms.

The school also added tennis. Most of the girls who joined the team had grown up playing at their parents' country clubs, which excluded me. Tennis was becoming popular on a national level. Billie Jean King agreed to play Bobby Riggs on television in September 1973. The match, dubbed "Battle of the Sexes," was a big deal. I'd never hit a ball before but fell in love with tennis that day. I made up my mind to learn how to play.

For me, it was amazing that Billie Jean had the chance to compete in a sport—let alone possibly beating a guy. This exhibition match mattered. I loved watching my brother compete, but I'd accepted that as a girl, I would always be an observer of sports—a second-class citizen. The closest I got was being a cheerleader in sixth grade. Billie Jean and Marvella showed me girls should think bigger. I'd ensure my daughters could play whatever sport their hearts desired. And attend any college. Why couldn't women be equal in athletics and academics? We were entitled.

Parenting books recommend that new moms nap when their babies do, but I used the time to study for the CPA exam while listening to Hadley's rhythmic breathing on the baby monitor. I passed the exam and interviewed to work part-year for Coopers and Lybrand (C&L), now PricewaterhouseCoopers (PwC). By working in the dreary winter months, I could earn desperately needed money and achieve some work-life balance. After my first "busy season," a C&L partner requested a meeting to reinforce my value to the firm.

"You know, we never hired an auditor part-year before. You were an experiment," he told me over an expensive lunch at the Columbia Club.

It wasn't the first time I'd heard those words, remembering when I was the first female hire in my department at NCR. And I was the only woman in the Club for lunch who wasn't a waitress. "I wasn't sure if the firm would be interested in someone who requested to only work mid-January through mid-April," I responded.

"We were intrigued by your cover letter. We just needed to know if you could commit to working at least ten hours daily during those three months. I commend you for proposing the arrangement," he said.

"I think it's a win-win," I said.

C&L paid me hourly for highly productive seasonal hours, 100 percent billable to the customer at a considerable markup. They didn't have to carry a salary year-round and didn't pay me any benefits. I was a cash cow for them. At least I was having a steak for lunch.

"We're going to expand and hire more pioneers like you next year in audit, and for tax too. In fact, we've discussed setting up a part-time partner track if you're interested," he offered.

I was shocked. "I'm flattered, but that would probably take forever, and I don't see myself doing public accounting work for that long." It took about ten years to make partner if you worked *full-time* year-round; at my rate, it would take forty years. I liked the clients and the accountants I met at C&L, but I found audit work repetitive and boring. I knew it wasn't for me.

"Well, then, we welcome you to continue as long as you'd like," he emphasized.

Later that day, in our kitchen, I told Scott, "Too bad both grandmothers don't think like the C&L partner. Your mom thinks it's irresponsible for me to work each winter. A disgrace to the family."

"True, but notice she and my dad don't offer any financial support during our lean years," Scott said. "At least your mom helps out a little bit with babysitting."

"Yes, but nothing regular. She's too busy globe-trotting. And I am happy for her," I said. Now that she was widowed, Mom had joined a travel club. I glanced at the postcards taped on the fridge. She'd sent them from hot springs in Iceland and hot air balloon rides in New Mexico. "She watched Dad travel all those years while she stayed home." Then I added, "Thank God for Catherine." A friend had agreed to watch Hadley alongside her own daughter while I worked those first few winters. Catherine made the whole thing possible.

Studying for the CPA exam paid off. Finances were tight with Scott's static salary and a growing family, and we counted on my part-time income to survive. Except for a few boring gray work suits, I didn't buy clothes for about ten years—not

Forget the Fairy Tale and Find Your Happiness

even underwear! For years, I handmade most Christmas gifts we gave family members, like tole-painted wooden Kleenex boxes or photographic gifts. We did set aside enough to buy a camcorder to capture Hadley's childhood on video. We also upgraded our home in anticipation of expanding our family, although that move saved money.

With mortgage rates down to around 7 percent instead of our current 14 percent rate, I calculated that we could afford a much larger house while reducing our monthly payment. We found a contractor to take our design and make it come alive. Scott and I had a strong nesting instinct, and having a beautiful home in a good school district for our children was essential. We opted to build in Carmel, Indiana, a suburb known for having the best schools in the state. We began constructing our dream house, but without any emergency funds or disposable income, it was financially scary, and there was no end in sight with a growing family.

"Do you think taking on additional responsibilities or putting in a little extra time might lead to a promotion or a bonus?" I hinted to Scott more than once.

"They already get eight hours a day out of me," he'd reply. "I don't want to become a workaholic like my dad." Scott went through the motions each day. His life would restart when the factory whistle blew each afternoon, and he'd return to his daughter and me, his best friend, before heading out for his daily run.

I began to accept that it would be up to me to earn the money we'd need to pay for our kids' college, let alone cars and clothes. A big splurge was a two-dollar Happy Meal for Hadley. I'd watch her eat it, then go home and make myself a peanut butter sandwich. This wasn't the traditional princess path I'd imagined; I'd thought my prince would be our provider, as my dad had been. Wasn't each generation supposed to be better off than the one before? It wouldn't be right for Scott and I to provide our kids less than we'd experienced. But without viable year-round day care options, my full-time work had to wait until the kids were old enough to be in school. We'd have to tread water financially until then.

"I guess I could teach one night a week," I said to Scott. I began a second part-time job, this one year-round, teaching managerial accounting at Indiana University's School of Business. I graded papers and planned lectures until the wee hours most nights while the family slept.

Making love with Scott felt like my third part-time job. Those two long years of infertility struggles had taken a toll. In college, we'd talked about having children but not about having sex. We were perfectly matched companions filled with deep love and affection. Still, even before we had kids, we lacked physical passion unless fueled by large quantities of alcohol, and there wasn't much of that since becoming parents. We centered our lives around Hadley. Somehow, our lack of money and lack of interest in sex didn't discourage us from wanting a second child. I wanted a sibling for Hadley. I think Scott wanted a boy. Neither of us wanted Hadley to be an only child. But mostly, that was society's expectation. You had two kids.

"Well, it only took six months to get pregnant the second time," I said to Scott.

"Cutting it a little close to finishing the new house before the baby comes," he replied.

"I think the house will win the race. This baby will undoubtedly arrive late, like Hadley." As an experienced mom, I thought I had the whole delivery thing figured out. My cockiness faded a few weeks before my due date when I learned the baby was breech.

"So Dr. Mackey wants to turn the baby to avoid a C-section?" Scott asked.

"Yes, but without any pain medication for this torture session."

I lay flat on my back in a hospital bed as two doctors pressed their four elbows into various positions across my oversized abdomen. I tried to dissociate my mind from this attack but couldn't hide the tears streaming from the corners of my closed eyes.

"The pain is all yours. The baby won't feel anything," the nurse tried to cheer me up.

"There's about a fifty percent chance the baby will stay head down after this procedure," Dr. Mackey said when he finally finished.

Why didn't he mention those poor odds before I let him pummel my stomach?

A few weeks later, the house won the race. I hoped lugging heavy boxes into our new home and pushing furniture around would jump-start labor. But no, my babies preferred the extended-stay option; my best mental strategy was acceptance. When Dr. Mackey ordered a stress test ten days after my due date, I decided to leave the "just-in-case bag" at home to keep expectations low for this latest trip to the hospital.

"Good news! Your placenta is healthy," the nurse said, removing the IV drip from my arm. "You can go back home.

We'll see you when the baby is ready!" She left with a click of the door.

I sat up and swung my legs over the hospital bed. As I stood to leave, a tidal wave of pain overcame me, and I buckled over. The stress test induced my labor.

"Scott, I think the baby *is* ready. But we have time. We must go home and call my mom to come. We have to get everything set up for Hadley. And we need the overnight bag. Then we can come back to the hospital," I whispered, doubled over with pain.

And Scott, the son of a doctor, did not overrule this risky plan. Instead, he pushed his wife, who was in labor in a wheelchair, out of the hospital to the car. "Looks like your pains are continuous," he noticed.

One painful car ride later, we arrived home, and I called my mom.

"I'll be there in an hour!" she said. Thank God *she* had her bag packed.

"Scott, we need to go back now. We can't wait on Mom. We can ask one of the new neighbors to watch Hadley until she gets here. This baby is coming very soon."

The furrows in his brow looked deeper than usual as he leaned forward, clutching the steering wheel with both hands. Despite facing a solid wall of pain, I comforted Scott as we headed back to the hospital.

"Don't worry," I said. "It's a well-traveled highway. We can flag down a policeman if we don't make it." What would have typically been said as an attempt at humor now seemed like a distinct possibility. Even lying sideways on the flattened seat, I could hear what seemed like every car on the highway passing us. I silently wished he would step on the gas for once. But not even the impending birth of a baby could speed that man up. He drove right at or under the speed limit the whole way.

Slowly but surely, we returned to the hospital. Now for my epidural! I'd have relief at last. More good news: My doctor happened to be on-site. Things were finally looking up. After a quick exam, he scooted his stool back and stood up to leave. "Everything looks fine. But your labor is too advanced for an epidural," he added, slipping out of the room like a coward. OBs are supposed to deliver babies, not bad news.

"Scott, he's kidding, right?" The thought of the relief from drugs, as I'd experienced with Hadley's birth, had been the only thing keeping me going through the painful round trip.

"Dr. Mackey doesn't kid around. Guess you shouldn't have left the hospital earlier today," Scott dared to say—as if he played no part in that stupid decision.

There was no energy for any negative thoughts. I'd require every ounce of strength to get through the delivery. I wished I were programmed to swear! Women are cursed! No, women are a *hell* of a lot stronger than men. There, I said it. One of the two cuss words I'd learned as a child but (no, Mom) I had never spoken until now. And no, Scott, I don't want any *damn* ice chips! That was the other one.

In the video of Tyler's birth, I murmured "a bouncing baby boy" after delivering my 10.5-pound son and then passed out. Tyler looked sunburned, and his skin was puffed and peeling, all signs of an overdue baby. He could've passed for a one-year-old with that head full of curly blond hair. I felt like this effort deserved some Guinness record. To this day, I don't know how I delivered him. I was a *badass*.

We had the perfect family—my prince and our little girl and boy together in a beautiful new palace in the suburbs, living the dream. But a few months later, I wondered if it was a dream that I couldn't lift my head. I lay face down on the floor of Tyler's nursery while he was sleeping and Hadley was at a play date. I wasn't asleep, but I couldn't get up. I just lay there.

"That doesn't sound like you," Scott said when I shared my scary experience with him.

"I know." Usually, I raced around, checking off items from my to-do list when he slept. But I was always tired with two kids and two part-time jobs. And I felt more overwhelming sadness once Tyler was a few months old. I was exhausted after the move, the difficult delivery, and taking care of a two-year-old and a newborn by myself. But I should have been feeling better by now. Thank God Tyler slept through this episode.

"Has this happened before?" Scott asked.

I shook my head. "But I don't want it to happen again. It was scary."

"Do you want to see a doctor?" he asked.

We had no money for an appointment with a psychologist, and insurance didn't cover mental health. But we agreed I should schedule an evening appointment right away. I figured there'd be some meds or earth-shattering psychoanalysis to solve my issue.

The doctor was Middle Eastern. I felt guilty about taking his time, worried he'd think I was some frivolous suburban homemaker because I had such a perfect life. He asked a bunch of questions and listened closely.

"You're probably suffering from postnatal depression, which is pretty common," he said.

"Is there a prescription for that?" I asked.

"Not for you," he laughed. "Simply start to exercise. Take a fitness class or take up a sport. Try to walk every evening."

That was it?

"Take time for yourself," he added.

This was a strange concept to me in 1986. But I went home and walked that evening after the kids were in bed. It was dark outside, but I didn't care. I was following the doctor's orders. And I *did* feel better. Better than I had felt in a long time.

We belonged to the YMCA so that Hadley could take swim classes, and I found some aerobic exercise classes that I could take in the evenings when I wasn't teaching or on weekends. I fell in love with this small escape and felt good about myself during and after each workout. Later, when Hadley started tennis lessons in a summer program at a local high school, I signed up too. I got my mojo back following those few shaky weeks. Exercise saved me. I felt stronger than ever. I finally got to do sports! Back to living the dream.

Lesson 6—Gender Matters

"Sam Simmermaker here, live on WCSI Radio, brought to you from Columbus, Indiana. It's summer in the sixties, and the hits keep spinning. We're at the grand opening of a home built for the future. Come for some lemonade. Stay for the tour. You'll marvel at the basement fallout shelter, built for the family to survive an enemy attack by the Soviets— nuclear protection for the nuclear family. You're listening to Percy Faith and his orchestra playing what else? 'Theme from *A Summer Place*.'"

The builder of the newly constructed home was hosting an open house next door. For the neighborhood kids, it was like having the State Fair in our backyard. I pulled my head back inside our second-story window, where I had a bird's-eye view of the futuristic model home and the festivities below. I'd been watching the building site from the room I shared with my older sister for months, anticipating when we could look inside.

I galloped down the stairs, my feet barely touching each step. Mommy was at the mirror by the front door, applying her lipstick from a shiny gold cylinder. She replaced the cap with a snap and pressed her lips tightly together before blotting them with one of Daddy's handkerchiefs. She took one last admiring look before facing my sister and me.

"Hold still," said Mommy, leaning down to retie the red ribbon in my hair. "Let's hope this stays in for a while."

We both knew it was probably futile. Mommy tried to dress her two daughters alike for church or special occasions, but she could always count on me, the youngest, to mess my hair or soil my matching outfit and ruin the Kodak moment she'd planned. Mommy looked beautiful, her dark brown hair styled in a French roll. She stood tall, graceful, almost regal. The grown-ups all said she "looked just like Jackie Kennedy." Mommy didn't like to hear that because "that woman is a *Democrat*."

She made one final adjustment to my hair and sent my sister and me out the door in matching red, white, and blue sailor dresses, saying, "God knows I've tried." Our first stop was the cotton candy machine. After a few bites, my teeth were red and a few pink tufts had attached themselves to my hair and begun to melt in the summer sun.

Forget the Fairy Tale and Find Your Happiness

My sister, Teresa, wanted nothing further to do with me. "I'm not holding your grubby hands. They won't even let you go in the open house now because you're a mess."

I wasn't quite five years old and figured I'd better stay with Teresa. I grabbed her dress with one sticky hand and followed her and the long trail of people into the shining new home. Teresa's favorite color was green. She was in heaven in the kitchen with avocado-colored appliances standing between bright orange Formica countertops. The fallout shelter in the basement was my highlight. An Office of Civil Defense film flickered on a screen as we followed the line of tourists down the basement stairs. A scary voice from the newsreel spoke about "nuclear blasts and radioactive fallout from a Communist attack."

Once downstairs, our guide pointed out some of the shelter's features. "Notice the sand on the floor in this part of the room. That *is* the bathroom. Just bury it! Never go upstairs and be exposed to the Soviets' dangerous radiation." Teresa must have heard enough because she bolted back up the stairs, but I wanted to learn more. "A homemaker can store canned goods on these built-in shelves and prepare meals for months down here, years!" the guide exclaimed. If only *our* basement were a fallout shelter, I thought.

The blaring radio station music beckoned me back upstairs. Looking out the family room window, I glimpsed some boys jumping on a trampoline built into a pit in the backyard and scrambled outside to take a turn. Teresa intercepted me and yanked me from the line. "You can't jump on it! It's only for boys today," she hissed in my ear. "You're wearing a dress; they could see your under-panties. And where's your ribbon?"

The ribbon was a lost cause, but I knew Mommy would never allow a boy to see our panties. Especially the delicate blue rose pair I wore today. That happened to girls only once they were married. I sat solemnly in the grass and watched the boys attempt somersaults and other stunts. The boys got all the fun. Girls were supposed to *watch* the boys do sports. I learned that lesson early.

No more sitting on the sidelines watching the boys have all the fun. Getting exercise was following the doctor's orders! Tennis lessons were followed by joining a ladies tennis team. These days, when I dove for a ball, the whole world could see my tennis underwear. We've come a long way, baby!

I didn't mind juggling part-time work so I could mostly stay home and care for my kids. I'd been dreaming about being a mom since I was a kid sitting alone in the designated corner of the family room where my toys were allowed. By age twelve, I'd become a popular babysitter, earning fifty cents an hour entertaining children. The moms of my neighborhood regulars said their kids demanded my services. I played with the kids instead of plopping them down in front of the television. We had fun.

"What adventure is in store for tomorrow?" Scott asked. He'd recently built a swing set in the backyard guaranteed to provide hours of entertainment, but he knew we were more likely heading out for some daily field trip.

"We need to round up some geodes for Hadley to take as collateral to the Swap Shop. I remember a spot near the creek where we can find a few." Indianapolis was home to the largest children's museum in the world, and we were frequent patrons. The Swap Shop was a "store" where kids could bring in an item they'd discovered in nature and trade for another.

"What's she in the market for? They're not likely to have any dinosaur bones, right?" Scott knew she was fascinated with dinosaurs and planets.

"No, and probably no meteorites in stock. Maybe an unusual bird feather or a sand dollar for the sandbox. Afterward, we'll hit the neighborhood pool and then make a library run."

"Another day in paradise. I wish I could join you," he said wistfully.

Even though he missed the daily educational opportunities I created for the kids, Scott was home from work in the early afternoon and used his time to invest in their athletic endeavors. It started when Hadley was only fifteen months old and still in diapers. Scott entered her in a running race—a 440-meter fun run for kids around a university track. Dressed in her lilac running jersey and laced up in a pair of Nikes, she received a white ribbon for finishing third in the two-and-under age group. Dad could not have been prouder.

Early participation in sports was the norm in Carmel, Indiana, where youth sport is a religion. The fields and gyms were packed with games every Saturday from sunrise until sunset. On weeknights, there were practices. As kids aged up, there were travel teams and weekends away. Scott and I wholeheartedly subscribed to this religion of youth sports. I'd been trained to observe sports, and now I could watch my kids do everything I'd always wanted to do. Raised with supreme reverence for the Olympics and respect for "the thrill of victory and the agony of defeat," both Scott and I loved Carmel's wide world of sports—it was the perfect environment in which to raise our family.

Scott was not your average soccer parent. It was his calling to be a youth coach. He was unpaid but worked nearly every afternoon and weekend for over a decade. He coached both Hadley's and Tyler's teams year after year. While Scott never managed employees in the office, he was like a CEO of youth soccer and planned schedules and drills with passion and factorylike perfection. He skillfully delegated other responsibilities to eager soccer moms, like scheduling game-day snacks and collecting for trophies and coaches' gifts for dozens of teams over the years.

There were many other sports besides soccer in Carmel, and we tried them all. During the preschool years, there were gymnastics and swimming lessons. After that, swim team; by age five, there were long weeknight swim meets in the summers. I volunteered Scott to be the starter. I can still hear his starter gun and his call of "Swimmers, take your mark!" We ended up with enough swim ribbons to wallpaper a ballroom. In spring and fall, we were on the soccer fields, with skating and basketball in the winter. Scott coached basketball too. Then there was football. Eventually, there would be hundreds of trophies, and we attended just as many sports banquets. Scott and I loved every minute; I think the kids did too.

Scott couldn't skate, so hockey was one of the few sports he didn't coach. But thank God he drove Tyler to most of those insanely early morning practices in the freezing cold. I attended the games, which took place at a more reasonable time, like 7:00 a.m. on Saturdays. The loud cowbells we clanged for good stops or shots on goal served as snooze alarms for some of us. It was too early to start drinking for warmth, and we jumped up and down to fight the frostbite. Living the dream.

Carmel wasn't only renowned for youth sports. It also boasted some of the best schools in the state. But preschool was our first academic decision. I was intrigued when reading about Butler University's Gifted Preschool in the Sunday paper. Hadley had started reading and writing books at an early age. Was she academically gifted? Probably many mothers wonder. I followed up on that article and took her to be tested. She nailed the interview, chatting with the program director, Marge Fadely, as if they were colleagues. Marge asked Hadley if she could draw a pentagon in a small space on the test papers.

"Do you want it to be a house?" Hadley asked as she began adding paned windows, doorknobs, and landscaping. "Should I put some people?" Without waiting for a response, she continued drawing. "The little girl is waiting on the porch for her best friend to come." She She added a blonde girl in a blue plaid skirt, with a pink top complete with a pocket, reading a book. Hadley was accepted to start in the fall.

The school believed in heavy parent participation. It was an environment in which Hadley and I both thrived. In time, I learned so much from the Butler University Gifted Preschool program that it felt like I had earned a master's in childhood development. It was worth the twice-daily hour-long round trips listening to Tom Chapin and Raffi cassette tapes on our commutes. I learned to value private education, even if it was only preschool. I knew our kids would go to public elementary and middle school. But maybe we could somehow afford a private high school to help prep them for the best colleges. My decision to stay home with the kids was starting to pay off by giving Hadley a great start—even if we had to dip into our home equity loan to pay for the schooling. ScottnDebt.

Everyone wants the best for their children—*better* than what they themselves experienced. I wanted my kids to have all the athletic and academic opportunities I didn't have—they deserved it. More than anything, I wanted my kids to be strong and independent—confident in carving their own paths to reach their full potential. As their primary teacher, it was my life's work.

CHAPTER 7

White Horses

Belle dared to be different. She struggled with the sameness of her provincial life and stuck her nose into a book to escape and dream of adventure—even if the townspeople thought this behavior was odd. Belle became the first Disney princess depicted as independent and intelligent. But she still needed a prince to reach her happily ever after.

It can be dangerous to be different. The alternative to taking the traditional princess path was not encouraging for women. Look what happened to female characters like Cinderella's evil stepmother, the wicked queen in Snow White, and Maleficent as they aged—they ended up bitter and alone.

While Mom followed the princess path, neither of my grandmothers was traditional. Both were single moms during the Great Depression. My maternal grandmother graduated from college and held a managerial position at a large utility company. My paternal grandmother remarried; she became a talented ceramicist and painter.

People described Dad's mom as "jazzy," maybe because her fingers glittered with diamond rings and she wore bright fuchsia dresses and bold necklaces. I loved spending time with her. Mama Dell gave me art lessons in her studio, surrounded by a warm kiln and shelves filled with hunks of raw clay and ceramic pieces in various stages of completion. She practiced painting flowers from her garden onto ceramic plates. The water lilies looked just like the ones in her Monet book. She refused to fly but said that if there were a way to *drive* to France, she'd make my (step)grandfather take us in their purple Cadillac to see Monet's lilies up close. And I would've had a window seat unlike trips in the family sedan where I sat up front on the "hump" between the parents.

My mom didn't allow us kids in the living room because the furniture was all white, and she feared we'd get it dirty. Nicknamed the "lightning room," my siblings spread the rumor that we would be struck by lightning if we snuck in. But Mama Dell's home was meant to be explored. She had a gilded mirror and vanity table overflowing with dozens of glass perfume bottles that had soft, round pump sprays, lipsticks in silver cases, and gold compacts with mirrors. She let me paint my dolls with makeup if I cleaned them off before going home. Sometimes she also let me paint myself. I spent hours sitting on that velvet chair playing with her makeup and trying on her costume jewelry.

As an artist, Mama Dell signed everything "E. Lane." Her real name was Eloise Lula Lane. Dad wanted to name me after her, but Mom said her name was too unusual. I don't think Mama Dell minded having a unique name. She *liked* things that were different, like her clocks. She had a sassy cuckoo clock, a loud grandfather clock, and an elaborate anniversary clock with a pendulum that spun around in a circle. Each hour, they created a chorus from different rooms.

    The best part about visiting Mama Dell was that she talked to me. I knew magic would happen as soon as I entered the back door and smelled the large gardenia bushes that crowded her breezeway.

For me, motherhood was a return to my childhood; spending time with my children felt more like a visit with Mama Dell. I'm not sure "stay-at-home mom" accurately described me. By now, I understood that my part-time work life would be short-lived, and I tried to maximize every moment with and for the kids before returning to an office full-time.

    Scott and I knew our kids would attend the highly ranked public schools in the area, but we learned the local elementary school didn't have computers for students. I read that IBM was wading into the school market. They were willing to fund an entire school computer lab at a few beta sites. I met with a representative from IBM and then arranged to visit an existing school lab. In consultation with the school's PTO president, I invited a school board member to join me. The next step was learning how to write a grant. IBM approved my submission, which thrilled all but one person, Hadley's principal, who preferred his school moms to limit their involvement to car pools and bake sales. I doubt he'd ever even used a computer.

    "Wait till he hears that I've alerted the newspaper about the grant," I confessed to Scott. "IBM wants some PR from this donation. That's the deal. Unless publicity appeals to Dr. York's ego, I'll never enter the computer lab." The principal didn't allow parents into the school as a general policy, but I just wanted a peek at that shiny new lab. "Maybe I can at least sneak into the gym's back door and watch the tennis." I'd just received approval for two other grants for the school—one for creative arts funding and another for tennis equipment and instruction under the United States Tennis Association's (USTA) school program. I was on a roll.

"You're not the average school mom. He doesn't know how to handle a woman that takes charge. It's a problem for him," Scott said.

"I'm just trying to whip this elementary school into shape for Hadley and Tyler; if they attend public schools, let's ensure they have an interesting experience."

"You were the one who insisted they go to private preschools. Now they'll think every school offers typing and French. Or you get maple syrup by tapping a tree," he said.

"Tyler's computer skills are already beyond most adults. His preschool teachers count on him to troubleshoot when the classroom computers are down. I have to do something. I can't let Hadley or our budding tech-support son down. I have zero regrets about the sacrifices made for their early education or my time writing grants. This is all about their future!" I said, the mom who dared to be different.

"Too bad you don't get paid for all your time," Scott added.

Sports were part of our daily regimen. We discovered a vast grassroots tennis program for Hadley at Scott's former high school. With thousands of students and more than thirty outdoor courts, there was a class for everyone and every level. All summer, from sunrise till sundown, you can hear the *thwack* of the balls at North Central.

Barbara Wynne founded the program by taking on the school district. Her heart was almost as big as her love for tennis. She never finished conversing with anyone without telling them, "I love you." Barbara wore bright-colored outfits like Mama Dell. She led the tennis program with great panache, although others did the work. Barbara's superpowers were fundraising and being a master recruiter of dedicated volunteers. She had an uncanny knack for trading favors to get things done—a free tennis lesson in exchange for a silent auction product donation or front-row seats to a pro event for corporate donors. Barbara hung out with Arthur Ashe and Billie Jean King and hosted a professional women's tennis tournament for the city, generating public interest in the sport. I responded well to her positive aura and love. I joined a women's tennis team at her private racquet club and tested my competitive chops. To borrow Barbara's favorite word, I *loved* it!

I was proud of the groundwork I'd laid for our kids' future and was having fun along this path. I was in the best physical shape of my life between the fitness classes and the tennis. I would've been perfectly happy to continue pouring my energy into improving the schools or growing community tennis like Barbara. But I had to return to the workforce to solve our family's long-term financial woes, confident I'd eventually work my way to the top. But for now, I'd climb the tennis ladder.

"Plantar fasciitis?" I asked.

"That's what the doctor called it. I call it the end of my running career," Scott said.

"But cutting back means minimizing the pain."

"Yes, I can still do some shorter distances, but that's no fun," he said.

"Is running ever fun?" I asked sincerely.

"When it's over. And you get to eat whatever you want without feeling guilty. All I do is sit at work . . ."

"But I thought you *loved* your job," I said, but my attempt at humor fell flat. Scott just limped over to his favorite chair and took a nap. He'd been doing that a lot lately. I wasn't sure how to cheer up my best friend. He wasn't interested in my new passion, tennis.

Scott's running injuries had piled up, and he'd gained weight. Scott hated his job, which was nothing new, but now he appeared to be genuinely depressed. This was difficult to understand because I'd grown up with a dad whose sole purpose was to provide for his family. I thought that's what every dad wanted—from Ward Cleaver to Charles Ingalls. This role was a cornerstone of society's princess path.

Several of Scott's best friends were now doctors and dentists like their fathers before them. A few more had taken the reins in their family businesses. The Joneses were all moving up. A nice home and good schools were table stakes for suburban life. Scott had been much happier in college when his doctor dad was his provider. Car. College. His bank account was always full. Today, his only joy came from counting the days until his retirement. Then he tried to move up the date.

"After you return to work and your salary catches up—which won't take long—maybe I can quit and manage the home front?" he offered.

I considered myself a supporter of feminists, fiercely favoring women's rights—in sports or in breaking the workplace glass ceiling. I would fight for my daughter to be whatever she wanted to be. Yet I resented Scott's desire to pursue a domestic lifestyle and didn't want to enable it. I admit that Scott would have been capable of caring for and handling children at home, and he would've been good at it. Picture a younger and more athletic version of Mr. Rogers. The problem was that this kind and gentle man was at odds with my expectations for a husband. He was no longer my knight in shining armor. My dad would have never allowed my mom to work. I silently blamed Scott's lackadaisical work ethic for our financial struggles—he was like an athlete who made no effort to win. I figured that if he hadn't received a promotion in ten years, it was his fault and it would never happen. I felt he'd let us down.

When I realized Scott was a mere mortal, I lost respect for him. He was no longer my prince on that white horse. And I needed him to be that man for me. I was so happy taking care of the kids, but he was taking away my happily ever after. He'd broken our contract, the social contract. I'd been groomed my entire life for the traditional princess path where the prince takes care of the family. But Scott didn't aspire to be a provider. He wanted to be a stay-at-home dad before there was such a thing. I couldn't handle that.

I also couldn't handle his morning routine. We stopped having sexual relations after we'd conceived Tyler. Scott had always been a morning riser, so to speak, while I was a night owl. Our body clocks had never been in sync, which gave me a built-in excuse for avoiding his sexual advances, and because of the kids, there was never a good time. He fell asleep when the kids did at 8:00 p.m., and I wasn't in the mood in the morning—I was always desperate for just a few more minutes of rest before beginning each long day chasing children. Scott would awaken early and enter our bathroom, always leaving the door ajar. It made more sense to close the door for privacy and to shield me from the light when I was presumably asleep in bed. I assume he wanted me to listen to him. But the sound of his morning ritual was torture. I no longer felt needed as a partner. I couldn't use earplugs because I needed to hear the kids if they awakened and called out to me. He would know I was awake if I moved my pillow over my head. I just lay there, wanting it to end—trying to be invisible. This routine went on for years. At some point, I began to silently cry each morning, sad at losing ScottnDeb. I knew it was physically over between the two of us. I needed to accept that this was what my future looked like. Cohabitation. What choice did I have? I didn't want to end up alone like my other grandmother, Mama Eva. I could almost smell that formaldehyde.

Lesson 7—Avoid the Old Maid

Mom said it would just be for one night—the only time I stayed with Mama Eva, my maternal grandmother. Teresa came with me, but I was still scared to death. The problem was the location. Her apartment was on the second floor of a funeral parlor. There were two ways to get to her unit. Mom took us the back way, up a shaky black metal fire escape. We'd smell that horrible smell as soon as we opened the door at the top of the rickety staircase. Mom explained that it was just chemicals from the business downstairs, but it smelled like dead people. Later, when we went for a walk, Mama Eva insisted we take the front entrance to her building.

"There are no more funerals today, and we won't bother anybody," she said, leading us through a long hallway. Then we walked silently down a thickly carpeted staircase to the lobby. Across the room, there were large, painted white doors. They were closed but undoubtedly led to the bodies. The awful smell was overwhelming. "Just pretend it's pickle juice, girls!" Mama Eva said.

I never saw Mama Eva without a smile. She was especially happy to have us sleep over that one time. There was no television, but we played the Old Maid card game about twenty times. It was a game that favored pairs. Teresa won most of the time as I kept getting stuck with the lone old maid card. I tried not to think about the dead bodies below when I went to bed that night. I reimagined the card game to strategize how to win next time. I didn't enjoy losing.

Mama Eva had a college education and enjoyed a professional career, unusual for her times, but she was forced to retire in her forties because she lost most of her hearing. Mom said Mama Eva had to live above the funeral home because she had no man. We were told her husband left before my mom was born, but I was never sure. Mom was adamant that Teresa and I needed to be virgins so there would be no "unwed mothers with bastard children." She avoided talking about Mama Eva's marital past, but Mom was crystal clear on one point: she didn't want to follow her mom's path. "My worst fear is ending up alone like Mama Eva with no man to support me."

That stay with Mama Eva reinforced Mom's message to me. I didn't want to be an old maid or live over a funeral parlor. I wanted an athletic prince to come along. I wanted intelligent kids and a nice house in a good school district with good sports teams. I also wanted to travel to other countries like Dad. I had to avoid the old maid to get to my happily ever after. I didn't want to end up penniless and alone.

When I worked before the kids were born, I was a rare female in the department. A few years later, at my part-year public accounting job, there were more women armed with college degrees and CPA certifications. While the workforce composition was changing, I still tried to be invisible as a working woman in the '80s. I believed that any hope of advancing in the workplace meant blending in with the males and not standing out. Any sign of femininity indicated weakness or suggested that you belonged in the secretarial ranks, and no one would take you seriously. Most professional women, at least in public accounting, followed the unwritten gender-neutral dress code and wore "uniforms" consisting of boring navy and gray suits with shoulder pads along with knee-length skirts, silk pussy bows, nude pantyhose, and coordinating pumps. Our behavior was expected to be just as bland and robotic. We held a poker face when we heard off-color jokes in the office, didn't speak about our kids unless asked, and quietly used a vacation day if we had to leave the office early to put out fires at home or attend to a sick child. Society expected women to stay in their lane and be grateful that they now had a lane.

No one was blander than Katherine, the senior who directed our team's audit fieldwork each winter. Katherine wore a pair of narrow wire-framed glasses that rested halfway down her thin nose; they functioned more like reading glasses most of the time. Her sharp, birdlike eyes scanned each worksheet bound in a manila folder before she added her tiny initials to the top corner to indicate approval. Page after page, folder after folder, Katherine worked with precision. When she spoke to one of us, she would nudge her glasses into place without blinking or showing emotion. She would address her concern with our work using carefully chosen and precisely spoken words, like an android. Katherine represented the type of mechanical female who could advance in the workplace.

As an auditor, I spent much time with Katherine and our teammates every winter. About ten of us sat in a conference room at long rows of tables for twelve hours daily, surrounded by stacks of legal-sized manila fastener file folders as we audited real estate partnerships. Food was delivered to keep the assembly line rolling, but sometimes we talked during our meals while continuing to tick and tie the client's books.

Except for Katherine, the members of our group were a few years younger than me—and maybe two-thirds were male. I was the only working mother. The other women spoke openly about plans for having children but were split on whether they'd return to the workforce. One or two eagerly asked me for tips on juggling work with pregnancy and toddlers. Like the guys, the other women had no plans to raise children and focused solely on their careers.

"There will be no kids for us," Katherine flatly stated. "My husband and I worked too hard to get where we are. We put ourselves through school. We work long hours. It's all we can do to take care of a cat."

"When you make partner someday, Katherine, you can upgrade to a dog because you'll be able to afford one of those dog walkers," one guy teased.

A few guys were married, and about half of their wives returned to work after having kids. "Unless I make partner someday, we'll still need that second paycheck to pay for private schools and a second home in Florida!"

"When I marry and have kids, my wife must work. It's the new American way. Both Joneses work—it's the *only* way to get ahead!" another said.

I reflected on those conversations on the drive home one cold January night after another marathon day auditing books. I realized it wasn't only Scott and me who faced changing gender norms in the '80s and their impact on the traditional family structure. As my coworkers mentioned, two-income families were becoming necessary to keep up financially if you wanted good schools and vacations. And I wanted it all. However, there was a difference between my coworkers and me. My husband lacked the ambition to advance in the workplace and earn these rewards. *He* wanted to stay at home.

I was the only car on the road, and my headlights cut sharply through the darkness. Snow flurries began to fall. It could be worse, I supposed. I could be taking care of the kids alone. After initially following Mom's path, I was now apparently destined to follow Mama Eva and become a full-time working mom. The main thing was for the kids to have a good

Forget the Fairy Tale and Find Your Happiness

life. Maybe being alone was not as bad as I'd thought when I was growing up. Mama Eva was one of the most positive people I had ever met, even if she did live over a funeral home. She didn't let that pickle juice get to her, even in death. She was cremated.

I pulled into the driveway of our beautiful suburban home, where we lived our provincial life. I loved our family very much, and while Scott no longer fit my definition of a prince, he was still my best friend. I figured we'd continue as platonic partners ever after. Or was there more to life?

January 2000

I opened my eyes to the sound of crunching glass. No prince awakened me from my deep slumber. Instead, a fireman stood on the hood of my car, carefully breaking through the windshield with an axe.

"Are you okay? Don't worry. We'll get you out. Just stay still."

I couldn't move anyway. Glittering glass shards covered my maroon Liz Claiborne suit. Snowflakes fell silently through the broken windshield, joining the glass. I was still seeing stars. It was strangely beautiful, this frozen white world.

"My phone is here somewhere. I need to call my kids."

"It's going to take a few hours, ma'am. We need to extract you first. But then you can call them."

Maybe now my husband would come. If ever there was a "white horse" moment, it was now. I needed him to swoop in and save the day—take care of me. Maybe Mom could call him. But she didn't even know he'd left us. I'd have to tell her now. I'd need her help with the kids. Anyway, she loved a good crisis. I closed my eyes and imagined his face. But my perky fireman was on a mission to keep me engaged.

"Keep your eyes closed while I finish up with the windshield," he said, about to bash in more glass with the butt of his axe. "You're not the only one to hit that black ice. Heck, a fire truck just went off this road on the other side of the river."

"I thought I was going to hit another car or the bridge," I said, wanting to open my eyes to inventory the latest round of glass shards.

"You're lucky you didn't hit anything except this little ole telephone pole. It's wrapped around your car pretty good—but kept you from ending up over there," he said, apparently referring to the dark, swirling water just a few yards away. "From what I can tell, the path you carved out here was good. You and your kids should be happy!"

Injured and stuck in a freezing ditch seemed about as far off the path to a happy place as I could be. I needed my husband. He'd take care of me. Somehow, I guess I still loved him. The white stars disappeared, and everything faded to black.

SECTION III

A Whole New World

Jasmine was a handful as a teenager. She snuck out of the palace to see the sights and broke tradition by challenging the sultan's plans for an arranged marriage. The first Disney princess not to be the main character or marry a royal, Jasmine was also the first non-white and Asian Disney princess.

Disney also broke ground with Pocahontas, a Native American princess and the first to be based on a historical character. In the movie, Pocahontas chooses to remain with her family over embarking on a happily ever after with her prince.

As it became more acceptable for women to join the workforce, many families embraced the two-paycheck lifestyle. Disney's portrayal of princesses during the '90s reflected this societal shift. Gone were the damsels in distress. Unlike their predecessors, these modern princesses answered the call to adventure. The winds of change opened a whole new world and gave women a fantastic point of view.

CHAPTER 8

The Russians Are Coming

The Disney princesses often demonstrated kindness to animals and strangers. Pocahontas took it to a whole new level. As the chief's daughter, she thought it was cool to meet people from different worlds and learn new languages and cultures. Willing to challenge her tribe's traditions, she went out on a limb and risked everything to aid a colonial "savage."

In the late '80s, the women's liberation movement continued to progress nationally. Closer to home, I was no longer the only neighborhood mom with a job. Abroad, there was another tectonic shift underway. Mikhail Gorbachev came to power in the USSR, and the world learned that *perestroika* and *glasnost* meant "restructuring" and "openness." The Berlin Wall fell in 1989, and Moscow's Red Square opened to tourists, including my tennis mentor, Barbara Wynne. She had a chance meeting with a Soviet tour guide, Valeria Titova, who shared a love of tennis. A former top player, Valeria offered to take Barbara on a

Forget the Fairy Tale and Find Your Happiness

side tour to watch some young Russians practice at the legendary Spartak Tennis Club.

"They have perfect technique! I want to learn how these coaches create such talent. We need this for *our* junior program," Barbara told me. "I'm not sure who had the idea first, but Valerie and I decided to organize a tennis exchange." The women planned to bring a team of young Soviet players and coaches to Indianapolis for the summer of 1990.

"I'm counting on you to help," Barbara said to her lieutenants when she looked for families to host the Russians. "Valerie will stay at my house, of course. She said the rest don't speak English, but they'll learn fast. It's only for six weeks. Love you!"

This was a lot to ask of the families. We eventually agreed to open our home when Barbara pushed hard for hosts. It was almost impossible to say no to her. Scott wasn't sure it was wise to associate with visitors from a Communist nation, but I didn't want to miss the chance for Hadley to meet a child from another country—especially one that might inspire her budding tennis game. I pictured we'd be paired with one of the young female players. We were surprised to learn we'd been assigned to host a coach for part of the summer.

"Debbie, I want you to meet your houseguest," said Barbara, pulling me inside the tennis house at the high school.

Barbara wove her way through the pack of kids in the hallway, pulling Tyler and me along. Once the coach spotted Barbara, he stood at attention next to Valeria, like he was in the military. His high, flat cheekbones gave him a distinctly non-American look—almost Asian. His tube socks were too long, and his shorts were too short for those skinny legs.

"Sergei, this is Debbie Miller. I love you both!" Barbara called over her shoulder before disappearing into the tennis office.

"Please call me Deb," I said. "And this is my son, Tyler. My daughter is on court."

Like all of the visiting Russians, Sergei didn't smile. That was one of the first things I noticed about them. In his case, it might've been due to his discolored teeth, the brown decay visible when he quietly spoke to Valeria in Russian instead of returning my greeting.

"Let's step outside; it's too crowded in here," said Valeria, leading us back outside.

Darn, I thought. *I wanted one of the Russian kids for Hadley.* Despite his stoic demeanor, Sergei looked like an athlete, tall with strong, broad shoulders, about my age. Through that longish Beatles hairstyle, it seemed like he was trying to steal a look at me. I smiled.

"He says you have the most unusual color of eyes he has ever seen," Valeria translated. "They look turquoise . . . Is that how you say it? Like water in the Caribbean."

I was wearing a neon green tank top over a black sports bra. The vibrant chartreuse color made my eyes more aqua than blue, especially in the bright sun. "Thanks," was all I could muster as she and Sergei continued to stare at me.

"Sergei doesn't speak any English. Maybe you can teach him."

I stopped to buy a Russian–English dictionary on my way home from tennis. If my family was going to host, we had to give our best effort. I knocked on the door of my neighbor,

Vika Farahan, who had immigrated from Russia. I wanted to learn how we could help Sergei and the rest of the team feel welcome.

"You are not Jewish," she said with a Russian accent. Her husband owned a successful rug company at the nearby Fashion Mall, but with only her head peering around the door, I wouldn't be glimpsing any of the rugs in their home today. "It is unusual for Americans like you to help Russians." It seemed like I was about to have the door slammed in my face. I must've appeared harmless, dressed in my tennis outfit, standing there with two young children, so she continued. "He could be KGB. These Russians probably think you are naive and will try to exploit you. Be careful," she added, her eyes big and round—bulging, as though she had a thyroid condition. She probably expected me to bolt.

When I didn't budge, her tone changed. "If you want to learn about that country, come to my class. I teach Russian culture at the community center on Thursday evenings. You can learn recipes and phrases—things to help them feel at home. And ask Indiana University if you can audit a Russian language class." She knew that, like her, I also taught there. With that, she closed the door, disappearing into her home.

Vika was right; I was a naive Midwestern housewife and young mother. But it was rewarding to assist those in need. I developed an urge to support as many Russians as possible. It started with Sergei, our assigned guest, and the other tennis team members spending their summer with strangers in a strange land. I expanded my network through contacts from the classes Vika recommended. Many attendees were aiding Jewish immigrants who were trying to assimilate into our country after years of what they described as repression. Those Russians needed everything from home furnishings to job leads. I also met some Americans at the university scrambling to go the other way—to begin a business in the Soviet Union.

"You are obsessed," Scott said about my efforts to help and absorb Russian culture.

"These people need me," I responded. He was probably right, but I never could do anything halfway. Every request was unique, and I enjoyed the challenge. This was a project I could do with the kids, and it didn't cost anything.

Lesson 8—Be Kind

Mom had a soft spot for strays—mostly cats and the occasional dog. They weren't allowed inside, but they could count on Mom for dishes of milk by the back door along with a square meal. She was also kind to strangers.

She'd say, "That's what ladies do," when asked why. Mom quickly volunteered for activities that got her out of the house. She was a Pink Lady at the hospital one evening a month and regularly visited little old women in nursing homes to cheer them up. She was a poll worker at elections. She helped at church with Vacation Bible School. She mostly enjoyed the social aspects of her volunteerism, and she dressed up for these outings with full hair and makeup, sometimes even wearing one of her fur coats in the winter.

Mom knew just what to do when Dad's cousins visited one Christmas. Their four kids were around my age and younger. She noticed they didn't have winter coats, boots, or even mittens, and snow was coming. She didn't take long to identify their sizes and head to the store. Their dad was a struggling minister, and their mom didn't work.

"We're using part of our Christmas fund for the Hueys this year," she said as we wrapped the mountain of gifts. "There won't be as much for you under the tree."

I didn't mind; I'd already planned to give them all my presents. They needed stuff more than I did. I knew the deal about Santa Claus, but those kids didn't. I wanted them to have the best Christmas ever. Thanks to Mom's kindness, they did. And so did I.

The local Jewish community did an excellent job of assimilating the influx of Russian immigrants. I rounded up clothing and furniture donations to assist their efforts. There was always something or someone to help. Assisting with the tennis exchange group checked off two boxes—it was the sweet spot that combined helping Russians and tennis.

Sergei became my special project. I was determined to help him learn English. He made little progress that summer, but it's possible he enjoyed my attempts. The crow's-feet crinkled around his eyes, and there'd be the slightest smile instead of his usually stoic expression when I tried my pidgin Russian each evening after he returned from coaching. Gradually, we pieced together his story with the help of the dictionary and Valeria as translator to fill in the gaps.

Like all Russian pros of the time, Sergei earned a college degree while playing pro tennis on the Soviet tour. It took players about eight years to complete a degree, double the average time, but it was considered a world-class education in sports science. Since Soviet players could not travel past the Iron Curtain to join the ATP or women's professional tours, they became coaches, earning a few more rubles with less effort and stress. We learned Sergei was not a member of the Communist party, but about a year ago, he *had* become a member of the recently revived Orthodox Church, proudly wearing a gold cross around his neck. He also had a family of four—a wife, a son about Hadley's age, and a daughter a few months younger than Tyler.

Their sport introduced the Russian players to a world outside the Iron Curtain when they came to Indianapolis that summer, and the tennis world was introduced to their talent. The genie was out of the bottle. Even their nine-year-old kids, including future greats Marat Safin and Anna Kournikova, regularly beat our Midwestern sixteen-year-old tournament players. I dreamed Hadley might play like that someday. After I opened my home and heart when I said yes to Barbara, tennis opened my eyes to a whole new world of possibilities.

CEOs also had trouble saying no to Barbara. She convinced American Trans Air (ATA) owner George Mikelsons, a local executive, to lend a charter jet to fly the Soviet tennis group to Florida for a vacation at her beach house. As a boy, George had fled Latvia before it became part of the Soviet Union. Barbara then asked for the ATA charter to fly the group to Washington, DC, before returning them to Indiana.

"I can't believe these Russians get to see the capital before our kids," grumbled Scott. "Not to mention a week at a mansion on the beach in Florida."

"Be happy for them! Maybe Hadley can have a similar experience over there someday."

"I'm not sure about that. It's a Communist country," he said.

"Maybe if you ever had a conversation with one of them, you'd realize they're not savages," I suggested.

It was sad to say goodbye to the Russians at the end of the summer. It had only been a few weeks, but I'd miss my nightly attempts at conversing with Sergei. Our guests were real people we'd learned to care for and about, not some Cold War enemies you see in a movie. Barbara must have said *"Ya lyublyu vas"* (I love you) a thousand times that summer. The host families hugged and promised to write. We'd barely said our goodbyes at the airport when Barbara made another request.

"Scott," I said, "I know we just had the Russians, but now Barbara needs host families for some teens from [the] Southern [district] next week—it's the Junior Hardcourt Nationals."

"I guess. At least they'll speak English," he said somewhat reluctantly.

Days later, Hadley gave a favorable account. "Dad! Hal and Walt gave me a free lesson today, and they hit with Mom!" Hadley reported. She was even more delighted later that fall when we got a call from Barbara to host some Women's Tennis Association players from Finland and New Zealand during her tournament.

"Will that be okay?" I asked Scott.

"Fine. Our first females. I like visitors from those non-Communist countries," he said, reinforcing his preference.

I loved each host experience. Our home had become a perfect tennis hostel. We inhabited the main floor but had two empty bedrooms and a bathroom upstairs. Since there was no language barrier, the whole family had connected with the recent groups. My accounting work took place during the winters, and with only one evening class to teach at the university, I had time to chauffeur the players and enjoy the cultural exchanges. It was exciting to root for our guests at their tournament matches. The kids also seemed to gain from each interaction. We looked at the globe and imagined visiting our guests someday.

Barbara returned to Russia that fall with her husband to begin plans for some American junior players to visit Russia the following summer—the second half of the exchange. I hoped Hadley might be chosen someday, and I volunteered to assist with the planning. Barbara hosted a dinner and shared photos and stories from her most recent trip to Moscow.

"Sergei was the best host! He drove John and me more than a thousand miles across the USSR to visit places on John's bucket list," Barbara said.

"Well, we survived," was John's explanation. "Sergei stored gas cans inside the van. There aren't superhighways with gas stations over there. It's a miracle we didn't blow ourselves to pieces."

Barbara painted her own vivid image of Sergei. Although she was about thirty years older than him, I think she had a slight crush on him. When she described how he ran alongside their train with tears streaming down his face as they departed Moscow on the Orient Express, I could almost hear "Lara's Theme" from *Doctor Zhivago*. What an epic love story.

The phone rang. Crackling, clicking, static. An operator with a Russian accent said, "Call for Deb Miller."

I instinctively moved into the pantry, what we called "the phone booth," so I could hear the operator over the chattering of kids at the kitchen table. Then I heard Sergei's deep voice. The connection was poor, and the English was broken, but it was him.

"Deb, sorry my English bad. I want study better. Then I talk you."

Suddenly, my body felt drained; with my back against the wall, I slowly slid to the pantry floor. Every fiber in my body froze, not wanting to miss a word. I thought I'd never see him again. This was like receiving a call from outer space. It must've been challenging for him to learn a new language. But now, it was difficult for me to find any words. I spoke with halting speech to ensure he could understand. "Sergei. You. Can. Speak. English."

"I try. Only you understand me. You speak 'easy English.'"

It was odd to hear him speak. All summer, he'd never uttered more than "sank you" now and then. I'd been the only one talking, trying out phrases I'd learned in my Russian language classes or reaching for the dictionary while he tried not to smile at my mispronunciations. Now, I was the one smiling at his efforts.

"Every day. Ten words. Bathroom mirror. *Leetle* yellow papers. I want speak good English."

It melted my heart. My student had been working hard!

"How are *you*?" he asked, followed by loud crackles on the line. I imagined both governments were listening in on this conversation.

"We are all fine." My whole body felt flushed. I felt dizzy, intoxicated yet drained. Hours later, there would be hives on my stomach. What was happening to me? I had no romantic feelings for a married man from Mars who had rotten teeth and didn't believe in deodorant. And I was pretty sure he smoked! But the idea that a girl from a small town in Southern Indiana was on the phone talking to a friend in another country was amazing to me.

"I practice more, and I come back," he declared. However, given how difficult it had been to organize the first trip, I wasn't sure that would be possible.

By now, the operator was speaking again. She'd never left the call. "Fifteen seconds."

I regained my composure and tried to speak clearly. "Sergei, we're sending Christmas presents for you and your family. I found someone traveling to Moscow, and they'll deliver."

"Sank you very much. See you in Amerika," he said, followed by one loud click.

I never told him about the hives. I never told anyone.

Sergei returned to the United States about a month later, during the holidays. He brought an artist named Larissa, and Valeria was their interpreter. There was also an older guy, Dmitry, who Sergei said was sent by the government as a "babysitter." *Great, now we're hosting the KGB*, I thought. Barbara hosted the females, and the men stayed in our upstairs guest rooms. Scott described our home as a Russian hotel.

The Russians brought crates of artwork on an Aeroflot flight to New York City, then negotiated with an airport limo taxi driver to drive them and the art to Indianapolis. It was the best way they could figure out how to get the shipment to the local gallery that had agreed to host a Russian art exhibition. I admired Sergei's problem-solving skills. But I didn't understand why he wanted to develop a business venture instead of leveraging his considerable tennis talent and knowledge. It soon became apparent he wanted my help.

Sergei knew I taught in the university's School of Business, and he assumed I was an expert in crafting business agreements. I tried to explain that I wasn't. All I wanted was for my family to have a cultural experience and maybe a few tennis hitting sessions in return for hosting the Russians. We hit a few times during his visit, and he reluctantly gave Hadley a lesson, but his heart wasn't in it. He borrowed Barbara's van and chased down every possible business lead he could pack into his short stay with the art exhibit.

Sergei wasn't the only Russian hungry to make business deals in America. As seventy years of pent-up demand for commerce was unleashed, there was a mad scramble by the few Russians who had privilege through political ties, government employment, or top athletic status to travel and buy or sell consumer goods. Gorbachev won the Nobel Peace Prize, and the Iron Curtain continued to crumble. A new breed of Russians emerged with their long-deprived entrepreneurial instincts on overdrive.

One minute it was art, and then Sergei wanted my help bringing the Bolshoi Ballet to the US. Next, he wanted me to meet an American who was trying to manufacture chairs with Russian wood for export. Then a Russian lawyer negotiating fishing rights for the Russian government wanted Sergei to help him sell caviar on the side. Many American businesspeople caught the fever and wanted to make connections. It was the Wild West.

I became a reluctant local clearinghouse for both sides, an accidental volunteer matchmaker for Indianapolis residents wishing to meet Russian business counterparts and vice versa. Big dreams and chaos. Some good guys and some bad. My head was spinning. During this mad scramble, I'd met an older gentleman named Dmitry Mikheyev through the university. He was a highly educated physicist and a senior researcher at the Hudson Institute in Indianapolis, a prominent public policy think tank.

"Scott, do you mind if we have Dmitry over for dinner this week to meet with these guys?"

He looked up from the weekly soccer schedule he was filling out for Hadley's team. "You mean the other Dmitry? The one living in Carmel, not the KGB guy staying with us?"

"Yes, he's the dissident who was imprisoned in a *gulag* for six years and then expelled and came to America. I want to hear his story."

"People will start thinking you're a spy," Scott said.

"I'll take that risk."

Scott signaled a thumbs-up. "Make it at eight p.m., though, and I'll miss the whole thing."

I was piecing together more of Sergei's story now that he could speak English. He preferred to talk about his latest get-rich-quick idea, but I wanted to hear about tennis. I felt privileged to have a historic peek behind the Iron Curtain. I knew Scott was tired of hearing anything about Russia, so we saved these conversations for later in the evening.

"Did your mom drive you to tennis?" I asked Sergei one night.

"No car. One hour go to courts on many buses. Mom never sees me practice or play. She makes tennis costumes only. From white sheet," Sergei said.

I couldn't imagine never seeing Hadley play a tournament, let alone practice. And you could forget about sewing tennis outfits. "How did you get started in tennis?"

"Before, I only play hockey winter, and we play *futbol*. We play every day. Outside apartment. So happy. One day tennis coaches come to the school. Gym class. To find best sportsmen. They invite my friend and I come to tennis. My friend wants go—I go too. He stop one month. I keep go." So, he started tennis for social reasons—to join a friend.

Larissa, the visiting artist, had a social request of her own. She asked Sergei to translate that she wanted to go to a club one night before they left. Indianapolis wasn't known for nightclubs, but some quick research revealed a DJ at the nearby Marriott. Sergei said he didn't dance and wanted to skip this event but was obligated to go as their driver. Scott had no interest in spending a late night out with Russians; however, I shared Larissa's enthusiasm. It was a chance for a night out, something Scott and I never did since having kids. Besides the wave of weddings that followed graduation, I hadn't danced since college. It was good timing; I was on holiday break from teaching at the university.

"Let me go first," Sergei said, pushing ahead in the lobby to the Marriott's "club." The music was so loud I could barely hear him.

"That man wants money. In Amerika!" Sergei shouted back over the noise.

"That's called a cover charge. Everybody pays to get in, like buying a ticket. It's not a bribe, if that's what you're getting at. Here, I've got it."

We snaked our way through the crowd to a table in the back corner of the club. Dmitry and Larissa tossed their coats into the booth and headed to the dance floor.

"You need beer, Deb," said Sergei, leaving me alone at the table with the loud Mariah Carey music. He returned, and we sat through a few more songs and another round. It was too loud to talk. I felt like we were the only ones in our seats. By the time the latest hit came on, "Everybody Dance Now," I'd had enough of sitting in the corner. I motioned for Sergei to follow me to the dance floor to join Dmitry and Larissa, and soon we were dancing to the beat. Well, I was dancing; Sergei, not so much. He watched me closely but his face was tight, as if he couldn't let on that he was having fun. At that moment, *Saturday Night Fever* spoke to me. It was like returning to Purdue in the Great Hall of the Beta house, only I didn't need a prince to save me anymore. My body just needed to move. I worked up a sweat after a few songs. It was glorious.

The music paused while the DJ spoke. Sergei grabbed my hand and yanked me through the crowded floor and back to our table. He'd had enough dancing.

"Too loud here!" he shouted over the din of the club.

"Why can't you enjoy yourself, even for a moment?" I asked.

"Why you smile so much?" he shouted.

"I haven't danced in years. It felt good!" I yelled back.

"I never saw you with red before," he said, pointing first to his lips and then to mine.

He'd only seen me in tennis outfits, exercise clothes, or jeans, without any makeup. Well, I was still in jeans, but it had been fun to get made up to go out for once. Hadley had helped Larissa and me to get ready. It was good for her to see a more feminine side of her mom.

Madonna was singing "Vogue," and the DJ started a strobe light. "We go *now*," Sergei said, rounding up Dmitry and Larissa from the dance floor. Sergei was tall and strong and spoke both languages with authority. He was the clear leader of our group, and what he said went. Larissa pouted next to me in the back seat of Barbara's van, but even a taste of fun was good enough for me. That night, I slept peacefully while dreams of moving to the beat danced in my head. I awakened with a smile as Hadley and Tyler danced on my bed.

Glasnost had opened up my world. We were pioneers on the cusp of something big globally, a once-in-a-lifetime experience. For Sergei, opening trade with America was the start of a giant gold rush. And for me, learning about a new culture was much better than reading books or watching television. I was living it. I felt more alive than I'd felt in years.

Sergei bought a fax machine for our home with proceeds from the exhibition. He said, "I send fax to you from my wife office. Fax free for me. Telephone call expensive." Unlike the summer tennis exchange experience, he viewed this visit to America as a business trip. I wished he'd stick with tennis coaching but understood that his whole world was changing as the Soviet Union seemed to be on the brink of collapse. After New Year's, the group flew home, leaving the Russian art that didn't sell in our basement. We'd gone from being a Russian hotel to a Russian warehouse.

Within days, a customer reached out to me. "The art gallery gave me your number. I hope you don't mind that I'm calling. But I must know, is that delicate hand-painted egg with the matryoshka doll painted on it still available?"

"You mean the nine-hundred-dollar one?" I asked, certain no one would pay that much for a tiny wooden egg.

"That's the one. I've thought it over, and I have to have it. It reminds me of my Russian grandmother," she said, not even attempting to negotiate the price.

I faxed the news to Sergei. His reply came a day later when I was up late grading papers. I could hear the fax machine beep and chug. I hoped it wouldn't wake Scott or the kids. Then it began to type, one line at a time popping up on the filmy paper. The machine shook on its small stand as it spit out the invitation required for a Russian business visa application with my name on it. The following line astounded me: *Buy ticket with egg money. See you in Moscow.*

CHAPTER 9

Have Passport, Will Travel

elle's fearless sense of adventure led her far beyond the village and into an unfamiliar world. It had been a long time since her hosts entertained outsiders, and they were anxious to impress. Belle earned their respect—and a seat at the table. Could she be the one to break the spell that had held them captive for years? There was only one catch: she'd have to tame the Beast.

"You'd think it would take longer to get a passport and a visa to a Communist country," Scott remarked.

"It was faster than organizing carpool support and explaining the kids' schedule to my mom so she can babysit while I'm in Russia," I added.

"It's only a week. We'll be fine," he said confidently.

I'd be fine too. I was excited to visit Russia, see the sights, and take a relaxing break from my busy life.

My first flight had been solo at age nine—I'd gone to see my cousins in Memphis. Mom and Dad were in San Francisco at a conference, so Mom's friend Patty took me to the airport. Patty cried when she handed me over to the flight attendant, but I couldn't wait. We stopped by the cockpit, and the pilot gave me a set of wings before I took my window seat.

I wouldn't be traveling alone to Moscow—not that I minded. Dmitry Mikheyev, the researcher from the Hudson Institute in Indianapolis, booked the same flight. He had his own itinerary but asked Sergei to arrange for his hotel in Moscow. Foreigners couldn't just reserve a room for themselves. Sergei probably had to ask three other Russians to assist. Nothing was easy in Russia in 1991.

Dmitry and an assortment of American businessmen made toasts and downed shots of vodka on the near-empty flight. With the country being under Gorbachev's control, Dmitry believed it was safe to return to Mother Russia following his deportation after spending years in the gulag. I'm sure this was the first of many celebrations he'd enjoy. No shots for me. Having some alone time was enough of a high—no one to cook for or clean up after or chauffeur for a week. I'd miss the kids and practicing with my tennis team, but I hoped I could hit with Sergei in Moscow. The back of the plane was empty, so I stretched out and tried to rest. I couldn't shake the feeling that I'd won a trip, even if it was to a dicey location. Given the growing unrest in the region since the fall of the Iron Curtain, Barbara was interested in my impression of whether it would be safe for the American kids to travel to Moscow that summer for the second half of the tennis exchange. I understood the concern as a parent, but I loved traveling and wanted my kids to see the world.

Forget the Fairy Tale and Find Your Happiness

Nine hours after our takeoff in New York, we touched down in Moscow. It was time to get the first stamp on my first passport. I peeked out the window at the desolate landscape along the runway as we arrived at Sheremetyevo International Airport; it was like landing on the moon—another world. I couldn't wait to explore this mysterious country.

As boisterous as the men had been on my flight, not one person spoke as we walked single file off the plane and down a long terminal corridor lit by a single light bulb. The only sound was the clicking of heels. My first impression of Communism was that they needed more lights. I imagined an interrogation room around the corner from the uniformed, grim-faced officials in Passport Control. What if these people thought I was a spy and wouldn't believe I was only a stay-at-home mom? The official inserted a piece of paper into my passport but didn't stamp it. Dmitry later explained that this was normal. But it seemed like I wasn't really there—like I was stuck in the Twilight Zone. I'd never felt further from the traditional princess path.

Sergei was about my dad's height and easy to spot in the crowd waiting outside customs. My eyes were drawn to his familiar face. But why was he holding flowers in his arms?

Dmitry pointed to the countless other bouquets in the crowd. "This is the customary way to greet any female at the airport."

Awkward, I thought, accepting the bright yellow and pink flowers wrapped in paper. I felt like a beauty pageant participant but didn't look like one after flying all night.

"Amerikan vooman!" Sergei said, flashing that big, squinty-eyed smile I'd only seen him use with Russians. I guess I'd been upgraded now that I'd made the trip. Sergei reeked of cologne, but it was an improvement over the sweaty tennis aroma and lack-of-deodorant smell I recalled from the summer. Sergei picked up my oversized bag with ease. In the States, I would have resisted—showing I was just as capable as any man of looking after myself. But after the long flight, it was a relief to clutch my flowers and follow along to the waiting car. I regained my urge to protest when the hotel registration clerk snatched my passport and left the area.

"Relax. Standard procedure," Dmitry said. "They will keep it until you check out."

It was scary having strangers hold my passport back to freedom. The bellman led Dmitry and me to the elevator while Sergei waited in the smoke-filled lobby. Only registered guests were allowed upstairs—so many rules and so much smoke. We were introduced to our second-floor "hall monitor," a woman who managed a large silver samovar and generally kept an eye on things in her ward. I smiled when she poured some tea for us, and I offered my best *spasiba* (thank you). There was no *pozhaluysta* (you're welcome) in reply. Instead, she began what seemed like a lecture. All those Russian language classes felt wasted as I couldn't understand a word. Dmitry was tired of playing translator and headed to his room at one end of a dark hallway. Getting this woman to return my smile wouldn't be easy. Smiles were few and far between in this country, but I took it as a personal challenge. And it had been drilled into me from an early age that a lady must wear a smile.

Lesson 9—A Smile Is Your Best Accessory

"Take the dry cleaning pile inside, please, Deb, while I turn the car around," Mom said.

I frowned as I returned from the drop-off. Running errands with Mom meant constant interruptions as I read my book in the back seat, and I wanted to register my displeasure.

"I hope you weren't rude to that clerk. A lady must always be polite." Then Mom talked about the importance of a smile and how far it could take you. "Dad told me it was my friendly smile that first attracted him to me," she said.

"Dad doesn't smile much, and he's successful," I pointed out.

"Men often wear a poker face, especially at work. But women have to look approachable. Because if a *woman* doesn't smile, men will think she's mad about something," Mom said.

"What if she's not *mad* but is just thinking about something?" I wondered aloud.

"Stop *over*thinking. It will give you lines on your forehead when you're older," Mom admonished. "Just smile! Put it on every day like an accessory you can't do without. And offer it to everyone, including to strangers," she added.

Now I was confused. "I thought we weren't supposed to talk to strangers."

"Who said anything about talking? If you smile first, they'll smile back," Mom said.

I was far from home in a country filled with strangers. They might not understand me, but I took Mom's advice. The least I could do was to appear friendly and smile at everyone, starting with the hall monitor. And she returned that smile—after I handed her a tip.

My room reeked of stale smoke. I looked around for a hidden camera and may have identified one near the top of the heavy curtains. Should I smile for the camera? No, I had to draw the line somewhere with this politeness thing. I was sure the phone was bugged too. When my doorknob slowly began to turn, I decided I'd seen too many Cold War movies. Fearless, I opened the door, expecting to find my nosy hall monitor peering through the keyhole. Instead, a small man speaking Russian motioned for me to come to the room directly across the hallway. I assumed he worked for the hotel and wanted me to change rooms. Maybe they had a nonsmoking room! I could see the hall monitor's silhouette observing from the lobby. Perhaps this was what she'd been trying to explain. It seemed impolite not to follow.

The moment the door closed behind me, I realized I shouldn't be in that room. How naive could a Midwestern tourist be? I turned to open the door but couldn't solve the foreign doorknob. The man was across the room by the heavy, closed draperies, talking in a low voice, pouring liquor into two crystal glasses. I pounded loudly on the door and called for help. He approached, speaking in Russian. When he tried to put his arm around me, I started screaming. Just then, the door opened as if by a miracle. Dmitry and the hall monitor were there. There was some shouting and the man stomped out, scolding the monitor as he passed. Dmitry exchanged a few words with the woman and slipped her some cash. Sergei was waiting downstairs. There was more shouting in the lobby when Dmitry brought him up to speed.

"Don't be mad at Dmitry; it was my fault," I tried to interject. I'd only been in the country for an hour and was already causing trouble for my host.

"You okay, Deb?" Sergei's face showed his concern about this situation. Seeing I wasn't upset, he turned his attention to the front desk, and his mood changed completely. He was shouting. For a moment, I thought he might attack the clerk. Dmitry explained that Sergei was demanding answers but knew they would never come. "No one admits to knowing anything in Russia. He wants to go upstairs and speak with the hall monitor," Dmitry translated. "I told him I already thanked her, but he seems to think she has more information."

Sergei's physical size was no match for the much-shorter clerk, who waved him over to the elevator. Dmitry and I remained downstairs, and I tried to reconcile what had just happened upstairs. "He was short; I'm half a foot taller than him. I could've knocked him down if it came to that."

Dmitry lamented how things hadn't changed as much as he'd hoped in Russia. "I should've warned you not to be so trusting. You're not in Indiana anymore, Deb."

"You not in America, Dmitry," said Sergei, smiling as he returned. Then, turning to me, he said, "And you need speak Russian." His tone was paternal. He lit a cigarette and recapped. The hotel *did* want me to change rooms, and the guy *did* work for the hotel, but he *was* a bad guy and would have taken advantage of the situation if I'd been willing. Sergei added that he'd paid off the hall monitor, so there'd be no more issues.

"What? Why on earth would you pay that woman? Again?"

"Beeznuss," he said, as if that explained things to me. Welcome to Russia.

After sitting through a few meetings that Sergei had arranged, I figured out that business was the primary reason Sergei had offered to use the proceeds from the $900 egg for my trip to Russia—the trip was not for me to be a tourist as I had imagined. I suppose I should've predicted this since he'd chased deals all over Indy during the holidays. At least Valeria and Sergei still planned to take me to the best tourist spots in Moscow as thanks for helping to host their previous trips to the States.

I dreaded breakfast. Each morning, a different bright-eyed guy would wait with Sergei in the hotel lobby to introduce a business idea to me while I ate. As we drove to a tourist spot, a different guy would appear and hop in the car to share a joint venture prospect. The presenters were always men. I didn't meet any women with get-rich-quick schemes to propose. Only once did a presentation take place in an office. The male presenter was running late, so Sergei and I sat in a waiting room facing the secretarial pool. The women I saw could be described as sexy secretaries, the type you might spot in a James Bond film with low necklines, short skirts, and bright red lips. I felt the urge to cough from the strong perfume smell that filled the room, rivaled only by Sergei's cologne. There were no typewriters, but they had televisions on their desks to pass the time. It gave me the impression that these girls had

Forget the Fairy Tale and Find Your Happiness

different job descriptions than their American counterparts, who were selected based on how many words per minute they could type. Perhaps these secretaries were hunting husbands—a Russian princess path.

Sergei leaned over to greet one young secretary by kissing her, touching her back, and whispering something in her ear. She smiled and lit a cigarette for him. The next thing I knew, Sergei and the secretary had parked me alone in a conference room. Not only was this rude, but if my suspicions were correct, Sergei's stallion-like behavior was unacceptable on many other levels for the woman, the workplace, and his wife.

"Where were you, Sergei?" I asked when he reappeared after a half hour.

"Beeznuss," he answered, his shaggy hair looking more disheveled than usual.

"It's not nice how you treated that woman," was all I could say. I wanted him to understand where I stood on this issue. "That doesn't happen in America," I added, hoping it was true and remembering that women had only recently solidified our position as professionals. It could damage the women's movement if young girls thought becoming a sex object was a better path than education and hard work. Women like me avoided appearing feminine in the office while trying to advance in a male-dominated world.

"Different culture," he replied. Indeed.

The male citizens of this Communist country certainly did not lack entrepreneurial instincts. The business proposals ranged from printing Orthodox icons on calendars to wooden toys manufactured from Russian timber for McDonald's Happy Meals. I had no interest in this and lacked both an industry Rolodex and consulting skills. But I wanted to be polite to my hosts. I smiled, listened to each wild idea, and gently tried to provide some leads. Each proposal was accompanied by a toast to future business. You could've filled a liquor store with all the bottles that were offered day and night. I'm sure the Russians were disappointed that I didn't join them in drinking hard liquor or smoking. I couldn't stand the way my hair smelled that whole week.

Each "beeznuss" presenter treated the opportunity to meet with me as if they had an audience with the pope. I didn't need a translator to understand their desperation. The future their society had prepared them for was now uncertain. They didn't want their daughters to be on the Russian secretarial path I'd witnessed. Like everyone, they wanted a better life for their children. I could relate to that sentiment. While I was exhausted from the hectic schedule, I knew I needed to listen with all my heart. Meeting someone from America gave them hope that the border would open fully and they could trade, travel, or watch genuine news programs.

We stopped by Larissa's studio, the artist whose painted egg had sponsored my trip. She proudly showed me the gigantic loom she had used to create tapestries that had been commissioned to decorate large concrete walls in entries of massive Soviet-style government buildings. I'd had no idea she was so talented. The art she'd brought to the States to peddle mostly consisted of traditional Russian souvenirs like matryoshka dolls, black lacquer boxes, and Gzhel china all made by other artists. In Moscow, she hosted a cocktail party in my honor where I met members of her artist community—Mama Dell would've loved this crowd. Larissa was dating an actor, Victor.

Forget the Fairy Tale and Find Your Happiness

Later, when I turned on the television in my hotel, I was surprised to see a younger Victor starring in a Soviet Western B movie. It was surreal.

Larissa's door was just a few steps from the iconic St. Basil's Cathedral; I felt like I was walking through a postcard when we strolled across Red Square. Valeria took me on a tour of the Kremlin museums where Russian royalty had once lived, complete with Fabergé eggs to admire.

"Why do all these people keep staring at me?" I asked. The locals seemed to know I was a fish out of water even when I wasn't speaking English. In Red Square, I was a prime target.

"*Amerikanka*," Sergei said.

"But how do they *know*?"

"You smile all time. Russians not smile many times," he said.

Russians smile when they get money, I thought, remembering the hall monitor. And who knows about that secretary?

I shared a genuine smile when I achieved my goal and was allowed to be a tourist. Other than the wacky business meetings, Valeria and Sergei treated me like a visiting princess. Neither was wealthy, but they were well-connected from their athletic status, and they took a page from Barbara and used favors or bartered to create a five-star tour of Moscow for me.

Valeria said females rarely drove in Moscow, so Sergei was our designated chauffeur, except for the time I left my hotel unchaperoned and took the subway for a ride around Moscow. My hosts were shocked and displeased when they learned about that side trip. But I could read Russian from my classes at the university, found their subway system easy to navigate, and was quite proud to get myself to the newly opened McDonald's at Pushkin Square.

Usually, fast food was not on the menu. We dined in a restaurant overlooking Red Square and at the Ukraine Hotel, near the Russian White House.. My favorite meal was a flaming pizza dish at a Georgian restaurant on Arbat Street.

"Sergei, this is the most delicious thing I've ever tasted! What is it?"

"*Khachapuri Adjaruli.* From by Black Sea. Goat cheese. You like it?" he asked.

"No, I love it." It was better than the best pizza I'd ever had.

"Then that is what beeznuss we will do, a Russian kitchen— in Amerika!"

I could've lost my appetite after hearing yet another scheme, but I shoved another piece of cholesterol into my mouth instead. It wouldn't be the worst business to have back home.

"I hope you like *Swan Lake*," said Valeria. Her son-in-law was a lead dancer in the Bolshoi. That night, we were front and center in the world-famous theater watching him perform. I was relieved to be carried away by Tchaikovsky's music and the beauty of the ballet for a few hours. I didn't have to speak or listen to a foreign language. Even better, it was the version of the ballet with the happy ending for the swan princess and the prince.

Valeria did not include Sergei in our evening at the ballet. She shooed him away and told him to see his family that night.

The two of them seemed to be competing over who could offer me the best experience.

"Deb, you don't like ballet and those museums and churches Valeria take you," Sergei said the next day. "*You* want play tennis!"

"No, I thought the ballet was great, Sergei," I said, trying to set the record straight. But he was right about me. Despite the beauty of dance and gold onion domes, I'd rather play tennis.

"Do you think we could see the tennis kids at Spartak? It's all Barbara talks about. I have to see it—and them. And I'd like to visit a Russian school, maybe your son's class?"

I was thrilled to reconnect with some of the kids from the tennis exchange and meet their parents at the legendary Spartak courts, but the two indoor courts were reserved for kids, and it was nearly impossible to find an open court anywhere in Moscow. Sergei held the USSR's prestigious Master Sport title and had previously been the director of a tennis club. He waved his magic wand and found court time for me with one of his former patrons.

"I thought this was just a hitting session, not some big competition," I said, not liking my odds playing a set against a stranger named Slava on his home court.

"*Ochen' interesno*," Sergei said—*Very interesting*. "Who will win?" He smiled, taking delight in watching two people who had taken up tennis as adults try to perform his sport.

"Slava make hotel for you and Dmitry," Sergei revealed. "Need government paper."

He implied that Slava, a budding Soviet diplomat, deserved a favor in return. Slava was stationed in Moscow after serving in the Russian consulate in Malaysia. Sergei had told him about the

Culver Academies, a boarding school in Indiana located on Lake Maxinkuckee. Slava wanted his daughter, Olga, to attend Culver's summer camp. Barbara and John owned a lake home there, and Sergei had spotted the camp the previous summer while the Russian tennis team swam and rode Jet Skis. A low-level diplomat, Slava didn't have funds to pay tuition; his daughter would need a scholarship. I put his request on my growing list. A daughter's education was a worthy cause, I thought. I'd win the set that day and, later, a scholarship for his daughter.

We stopped by a school on my last day in Russia. I spoke slowly to Sergei's son as we left the class, hoping he'd understand. "Thank you, Andre. It was nice to meet you, your teacher, and the students. I know the kids in my daughter's class in the US are looking forward to the pen pal letters. I appreciate your dad arranging this."

"He's not my dad," the boy said in decent English. His face was emotionless. It turned out that Sergei didn't have a son. He later explained that Andre was his wife's son from her first marriage. Maybe that's why the boy seemed cold toward Sergei. What other secrets was he keeping from me? I thought we'd become close friends, but it was odd that I hadn't met the rest of Sergei's family this week. On our drive to the airport, I asked why.

"Apartment long drive. My little daughter go early sleep," he said.

"But doesn't your mother-in-law live with you? Couldn't she babysit so your wife could join us one evening? Or Andre could babysit. He's old enough."

"This is beeznuss. Woman not come to beeznuss." He lit another cigarette.

Forget the Fairy Tale and Find Your Happiness

Oh my God. What a beast! Which part of that sexist comment should be attacked first? Between the smoky car rides, smoke-filled meetings, and restaurants, my sense of smell had also had enough. "What does your wife think of your smoking?" I asked, remembering how much Mom detested Dad's habit, which probably contributed to his cancer and premature death. Mom used to say Dad had to brush his teeth before he could get near her.

"She smokes," he responded.

Sergei didn't smoke inside our house either time he stayed, but he reeked of smoke many times. I didn't like my kids being exposed even indirectly to the smoke or the habit. I decided to make a stand. I reached over, grabbed his pack of cigarettes from the car console, and dumped the remaining ones into my lap. He didn't try to stop me.

"Sergei, you've seen that no one smokes in America anymore. You must stop smoking if you want my help with your business ideas and if you ever expect to stay at our home again." I crisply broke each cigarette in half, one by one. I was committed to taming the beast. He shook his head, but I noticed a sly smile. He seemed to accept my challenge.

"Crazy Amerikan vooman!" he said with a smile.

So, he did consider me a woman. But I guess he had different boundaries for *American* women. We could drive and attend business meetings. And we didn't light cigarettes for men; we broke them.

"Different culture," I replied. Indeed.

A few weeks after I returned to Indiana, student pen pal letters from the school in Moscow began to arrive. Hadley's teacher invited me to visit the kids and share some of my cultural experiences and souvenirs.

"Do you guys want to learn to say something important in Russian?" I asked Hadley's class.

"Yes!"

"Okay, I'll teach it using some English words that sound the same. What color is this?" I pointed to a flower on my shirt.

"Yellow!" they shouted in unison.

"And this color?" I asked, pointing to my jeans.

"Blue!"

"And can you tell me what this is?"

"A vase of flowers!" they shouted.

"Good work. Let's combine these by saying the three keywords—the two colors and the word 'vase.' Only pronounce 'vase' like your rich aunt in New York would, and say it like, 'vaas.'" They giggled as Hadley and I practiced to demonstrate. "Now, let's practice it all together. Turn and face the person next to you." They all turned immediately. "Look them in the eyes, and on the count of three, everybody say those three magic words."

"Yel-low-blue-vaas!" they screamed at each other.

"Perfect! You just said 'I love you' to your neighbor." I smiled. The boys groaned and the girls gleamed, especially Hadley, who was in on the joke. "*Ya lyu-blyu vas* is one way to say 'I love you' in Russian. I hope you enjoyed this presentation as much as I loved my trip to Moscow."

Back in Indiana, I was seen as a (mostly) stay-at-home mom whose only presentations were in classrooms. But despite the sexism, I'd been accepted as a respected businessperson in Russia. I had the credentials and a passport to a new world with real people beyond books or my comfort zone. These people needed help to overcome their recent hardships. My provincial life had suddenly become *ochen' interesno*.

CHAPTER 10

Back Home in Indiana

Mulan took a risk when she joined the military. After a rough start, she ultimately brought honor to her family. Mulan was strategic and smart; the emperor and others recognized her strengths even before she did. A female leader? Imagine that.

From the safety of our couch, Hadley, Tyler, and I watched the television as tanks rolled past the Russian White House, where I'd strolled just a few months before. It had been an excellent decision to keep the American tennis kids away from Moscow in the summer of 1991.

Soon after my return from Russia, the parents from Barbara's tennis program became nervous about sending their kids to the USSR for part two of the Indianapolis-Moscow Tennis Exchange. Barbara and Valeria postponed the Moscow trip and instead brought the Russians back to the US for a second consecutive summer. Kournikova didn't return as she'd earned

Forget the Fairy Tale and Find Your Happiness

a free ride to Nick Bollettieri's tennis academy—the most famous in the world—but Sergei returned as a coach.

"I promised Sergei that if he stopped smoking, he'd have a place in our home."

"Oh, he feels at home all right," Scott replied. "What does your mom think about him staying here again this summer?"

"She *likes* the Russians. Don't you remember how she fussed all over them at Christmas? She can socialize with anyone."

"Even socialists," he muttered.

"Good one. Mom thinks I'm in love with tennis," I said. "No pun intended."

"Ha-ha," he said. "Well, you *are* addicted to the sport."

"I love my tennis team—the practices, the matches. And watching Hadley is the best. Stressful during tournaments, but I can see her confidence growing. She's such a strategist. And now Tyler is playing in the Summer Wonders group!"

"I think he should stick to ice hockey," Scott said.

"I don't think tennis is his sport, but he sure liked hanging out at the ATP event this summer . . . one of the perks of having a former pro player staying at our home," I added. Scott didn't share my interest in tennis. He didn't understand the joy I felt when Sergei's friends, Russian pros playing in the tournament, gave our family tickets to the ATP men's tennis tournament in Indy. Sergei had arranged a credential for me that allowed me to dine with the pros, their families, and their coaches and gain behind-the-scenes experience. It was a dream week for me, but Scott wasn't impressed to hear that we'd hung out in the player lounge—near Agassi and Courier—or that I'd sat courtside and watched Boris Becker, fresh from his win at Wimbledon, lose to Pete Sampras, my tennis idol, in the final. But when the Soviet coup attempt in late August delayed Sergei's return to Moscow, Scott was ready to stage his own rebellion.

"You've got to be kidding me. What's next? Barbara moves him here permanently?" he asked.

"Scott, have a heart. Sergei's country is falling apart, and he can't even get through by phone to check on his family's safety. He'll leave as soon as flights begin again."

Unlike Scott, I valued my friendship with Sergei. It was easy to communicate with him now that he could speak English. Barbara kept him busy all summer with coaching and driving the Russian kids to tournaments across the Midwest every weekend. We rarely saw him. However, he could still squeeze in some meetings with potential business partners. I had a feeling he'd be even more interested in business now that Gorbachev was out, Yeltsin was in, and the USSR had dissolved. Soon, the tanks disappeared, Sergei returned to Moscow, and Russia officially opened for business.

I was hopeful that America and Russia could become friends. The people I'd met there desperately wanted to trade with Americans. Their confidence in me as a potential business partner was inspiring. The tennis exchange proved it was possible to organize a project between the two countries. Maybe another wild idea *could* work. Through my teaching position in the School of Business for Indiana University, I connected with a few prominent companies that had serious interests in Russia, including Cummins, Mayflower, and Firestone Building Products. I wanted to pick their brains about this potential marketplace. While still politely sifting through the flood of small business ideas from Sergei's faxes, I began focusing on a few larger opportunities that might have merit. The opening of trade with Russia felt like history was being written.

I received a call one day from Bernie, a local businessperson who was working on a deal with Anheuser-Busch (AB) for the distribution rights to sell Budweiser beer in Moscow. He'd met with Sergei the past summer and was interested in hiring me to do some financial research to support the project. I was intrigued. Maybe this would be that one-hit song. The opportunity became real when Bernie invited me to St. Louis to meet with AB's marketing team. We flew on a private jet Bernie had arranged along with a team from the Mayflower shipping company and their important Russian guest, Mr. Tatashvili, CEO of Sovtransavto, a large trucking company in Russia. Bernie envisioned that these companies would support his beer distribution project. The AB meeting went well, and the next step was for me to go to Russia to conduct some financial fieldwork. Bernie asked Sergei to make the arrangements in Moscow for hosting AB's director of international marketing and me. This time, I would visit Russia as a businessperson, with no intentions of being a tourist.

Scott's patience was growing thin with my Russian adventures. He hadn't seen how desperate the situation was for the people I'd met in Russia, and he did not find it rewarding to help them. Additionally, he wasn't into tennis and would have preferred it if Hadley stuck with soccer or took up cross-country running. But Scott agreed that the AB project was an opportunity for me to finally be compensated for my efforts. I figured it could also provide some international experience for my résumé, which would be helpful since Tyler would be in school in about a year and I'd soon return to work full-time.

When I flew to Moscow to do the AB work, I wore casual attire—pink floral pants. As much as I liked the pants, I wanted to burn them by the end of the trip. Delta Airlines lost my luggage on the flight over. I wore those pants daily for the next three weeks. I opened every business appointment with my apologies. There was nothing to buy in Moscow for a thin six-foot-tall woman. Floral pants or not, I had a productive time in Moscow. I felt fierce and free—like I could conquer anything.

Sergei and I were a team. He organized all the meetings I attended to collect data for the AB project. Sergei would do anything for his friends. During my stay, his friend Oleg asked him to collect a file from Oleg's office at the legendary Peking Hotel. The door was locked, but that wouldn't stop Sergei. I knew Sergei would find a way to deliver. When the hotel staff failed to produce a key, he stormed down the hall and grabbed an axe from the fire alarm box. I watched, horrified, as Sergei chopped down the ten-foot-tall vintage wooden door. The man had a temper and would never disappoint a friend.

Sergei was convinced that real estate was the best investment in Moscow. Following the collapse of the Soviet Union, Russia allowed the sale of apartments, and Sergei predicted the prices would skyrocket as Western businesspeople flooded the area and needed housing. The numbers he shared were convincing. When I returned home, I compared notes with my US contacts who were doing business in Moscow. They were considering or already making similar investments. Even Scott agreed this was a good idea. We borrowed money from our home equity and wired it overseas. We provided most of the funding per our contract, but Sergei did the legwork. He agreed to quickly repay us for the bank loan using future rental income, and we were to share equally in the profits upon the unit's eventual resale. It looked like my efforts with Russia were beginning to pay off.

Bernie didn't join me in Russia, but he gobbled up the financial analysis I'd collected in Moscow. Both he and AB in St. Louis were pleased, but I was surprised when Bernie invited me to expand the scope of the engagement to include some marketing research. I tried to talk him out of it at first. I'd taken marketing classes for my MBA and my undergrad degree in management, but I had no marketing experience. I'd spent six years in corporate finance, five years doing part-time CPA work, and taught accounting at Indiana University. Why me?

"You know how to communicate with these people. That's priceless," Bernie said. He must've recognized the value of the relationships I'd built through the fieldwork.

Sergei insisted I accept. "These retailers in Russia only trust you, Amerikan vooman!" Bernie promised Sergei a piece of the ongoing business once the deal was completed. Until that point, Sergei continued to donate his efforts. He counted on me to seal the deal.

I accepted the additional challenge under the condition that I could complete most of the work from the States to be with the kids. The only red flag was that Bernie said he couldn't pay me until the deal was signed with AB that summer. I opted not to teach at the university that semester and skipped the accounting work to focus on the AB project. Waiting to be paid was disappointing, but I could work around the kids' schedules. No corporate job could offer that to me in 1992. The marketing research I compiled was well received. Bernie and AB were set to sign the final agreement in the summer and launch operations immediately.

I developed the public relations plan with AB and was expected to return to Moscow to coordinate the on-site portion of the signing event. To soften the blow of my second absence for the AB project, we arranged for Scott to fly to Colorado with the kids and take a vacation with his sister, Suzy, and her family. After the signing, we'd have plenty of money to cover this splurge. I'd miss going along, but we all had something to look forward to that summer.

Bernie couldn't make the trip, but he gave me a bunch of AB swag to take to Moscow for the signing. I couldn't wait to hand it out to all the Russians who had helped me with this project. While Bernie paid for my flights, Sergei and his friends covered my hotel charges, meals, and ground transportation for both trips. The Russians also arranged my meetings with the potential customers. I couldn't have done it without them, especially Sergei. I put the finishing touches on the PR plan and packed a bag. I was excited to see the project come to fruition in person. This would be a significant event for Russian-American business, and I was a big part of it.

Unfortunately for all of us, Bernie didn't do *his* part. Bernie failed to provide his required investment as part of the contract with AB, and they canceled the deal—and the signing. I learned this right after landing in Moscow, while holding the bag full of AB swag.

Although AB soon continued the project with another partner, I felt like a failure. Without a signed deal, I wasn't sure when or if Bernie would pay me. More importantly, I felt like

Forget the Fairy Tale and Find Your Happiness

I'd let down the people in Moscow who had supported the project. I didn't think I could ever look at another Budweiser beer bottle in the same way. Until this experience, I'd thought hard work always paid off. I returned home empty-handed after six months of effort and was ready to leave Russia behind—no more speculation. I liked a secure paycheck. And I didn't want to fail people.

When one door closes, another one opens. This time, my tennis fairy godmother came calling. Days after I returned from Russia, Barbara reached out. She ran the nonprofit that owned Indy's women's pro tennis event. The nonprofit had planned to sell the event and use the proceeds to start a scholarship fund for Indianapolis junior tennis players, but the deal fell through. That meant the nonprofit would be liable for hundreds of thousands in event prize money even if they canceled, and they'd lose the right to sell the event in the future if it wasn't held. Usually, a small staff worked year-round to stage the event. They'd disbanded nearly a year ago.

"The tournament is back on, and you're leading it. We've got a meeting with WTA tournament directors at the US Open in New York. Start packing!" Barbara said.

"But what do I know about leading a women's pro tennis event?"

"You have two business degrees, and you teach it. You organized a beer venture with Anheuser-Busch in Russia. You can do anything!" Barbara continued, "You're just the right one to lead us out of this financial mess. You'll have to work fast. We have only two months to do the work. We have more than a hundred volunteers lined up. They'll help."

"But Barbara, I've never managed employees. Why don't you do it?"

"We'll pay you!" Barbara said. "And I'm too old, anyway."

"You're ageless, Barbara," I replied.

"See? You're a natural for the PR part." She leaned in and squeezed my arm. "Age is irrelevant. You're ready for this. Love you!"

Lesson 10—Age Is Only a Number

"Take the key," Dad said.

"I'm only eleven."

"Age is only a number," Dad replied, offering me the key to our boat. "I drove a tractor when I was younger than you. They told me I was ready," he said with a faraway look. Dad didn't talk much about his childhood.

All summer, Dad had been training me to drive water-skiers and dock the boat carefully. I knew how to put gas in and how to use the choke to start a cold engine. I guess I'd passed his test. He wouldn't say I was ready unless it was true.

"But what about Teresa? She's fourteen." My sister was older than me but had never touched the keys. Until that moment, I figured only my brothers got to drive the boat—not the girls. I doubted Teresa had any interest. Lately, she hadn't visited the lake; she had stayed home and missed the fun. I didn't mind because it meant I got to bring a friend. But ever since Teresa's childhood illness, I'd felt it was my duty to look out for my sister.

"Don't worry about anyone else. *You're* ready," he said.

I reached over and took the boat key. I was going to command my own ship!

"Just don't ever give the Lake Patrol any reason to call me about your driving," he added.

Barbara was one of the first non-Russians to see me as a businessperson. When she invited me to become the tournament director of the Indianapolis women's pro tennis event, she rewarded me with an opportunity to put my business skills to work in combination with the sport I loved. Barbara wanted to minimize the losses and stage the event one last time so the nonprofit could sell it once and for all to establish the tennis scholarship funds. She believed in me.

I didn't let Barbara down. We raised hundreds of thousands of dollars from sponsors, and I managed forty committees. The PR experience I'd gained from the AB project was valuable in coordinating the international media covering the event. Barbara loaned me a huge office fit for the CEO of a major company within her husband's luxurious office complex and arranged for his personal secretary to provide me with admin services. I'd never had a secretary before, but she was highly skilled and taught me how to leverage her support into a fantastic resource for the tournament.

I didn't miss a beat at home. The hours when my kids were at school were packed with meetings and calls in the office. I'd start work again at home after they went to bed and into the wee hours of the night.

"I've always been amazed how you can operate with so little sleep," Scott remarked.

"That's what it takes to get the job done," I said. The only gear I had was full speed. I loved every second of it.

All fall, while I was having the time of my life organizing the women's tennis event, Sergei was struggling back in Russia. A year after the dissolution of the Soviet Union, life had become challenging for its citizens. The country was on the road to democracy without knowing how to get there, resulting in chaos, unprecedented crime, and economic collapse. Like many, Sergei had lost his life savings overnight and was becoming more desperate by the moment. It didn't help that the AB deal had been a professional embarrassment. Unlike Sergei, I could leave it behind in Russia. Then his personal life became unhinged when his wife asked him to leave.

"No live good in home. I sleep in bathtub, and she don't want our daughter," Sergei said by phone about his wife. "I want move to America with my daughter. Can you help me?"

I imagined he would struggle as a single father and knew he wanted Lina to have a better life than Russia could offer at that time. Sergei regularly expressed how much he wanted her to grow up in America. He assured me his wife agreed that a move to the US would be best for their child. I would do anything for my kids to have a promising future, so this rang true. But I felt guilty about how perfect my professional life had become while his opportunities had dried up. Yet relocating Sergei and Lina to America seemed like a big project even for me.

Cast out by his wife, Sergei struggled to find a place to live in Moscow. Without telling me, he and Lina moved into the Moscow apartment Scott and I had financed with a loan from

Forget the Fairy Tale and Find Your Happiness

our bank. That meant the unit didn't have any paying tenants as agreed. Scott and I were effectively funding Sergei's housing and were not likely to receive the repayment of the loan or the planned return on our investment anytime soon. I was not pleased to uncover this news. Scott would have a fit. But I had an idea of how to solve this financial challenge.

"Scott, what if they stayed upstairs?" I'd asked my husband before taking the idea any further. "Sergei wants to raise his daughter in America. I'm sure the racquet club would give him a job. It would only be until he can get on his feet. You know Hadley and Tyler would enjoy having another kid in the house," I said. Scott had to support the idea or it wouldn't work.

"Okay. You should be in marketing after the tournament, or sales," Scott said.

Problem solved. We could rent out the Russian apartment after all. And it was the right thing to do to help my friend. I just hoped the green card process wouldn't take long. Taking a page out of Barbara's playbook, I contacted a few airlines, and TWA agreed to donate two tickets from Moscow to Indy in exchange for some PR at the tournament. The Russians were coming. Barbara was in for a big, but hopefully welcome, surprise.

The weeklong pro tennis event arrived after a few demanding months of planning. Hadley and Tyler were proud to call their mom the tournament director, and they enjoyed hanging out in the player lounge and watching the matches from box seats. Mom surprised me when she stopped by one day. But instead of watching a match, she collected a stack of event programs.

"Some of my friends still play tennis at the country club. They'll enjoy reading about my daughter—the director," she said proudly. "You know I played tennis when I was a girl."

At the closing ceremonies, it was my turn to surprise Barbara. Surrounded by sponsor banners, we went onstage to hand out the trophies.

"I didn't know you'd lined up TWA as a sponsor," Barbara remarked about the airline's banner.

"I'll explain later, Barbara," I said, amazed she'd spotted that minor detail.

"This is the saddest day ever," Barbara said. It was emotional for her to preside over the last women's pro event in the city. She felt she'd let down the sport and the city of Indianapolis by selling the event. Right after we handed out the trophies, I held onto the microphone.

"We've got one more announcement. Compliments of TWA, two special guests are in attendance as a surprise for Barbara, who brought us women's professional tennis over the years and co-founded the Indianapolis-Moscow tennis exchange." It was Sergei, back in Indiana, this time with his young daughter, Lina, right off their flight from Moscow. As predicted, Barbara was delighted and jumped at the chance to have a top Russian coaching in Indianapolis year-round. She was thrilled to support Sergei's relocation project and persuaded her son's legal practice to prepare the immigration papers pro bono.

"You're changing people's lives, Deb," Barbara said. "I am so proud of you. I'll bet Hadley and Tyler are too."

Barbara and tennis had undoubtedly changed my life—and Sergei's. He was beginning his new life in America, but

Forget the Fairy Tale and Find Your Happiness

the tennis tournament was over for me. The most fun job I'd ever had ended much too quickly. It sure beat my previous corporate finance jobs and the long, tedious hours of CPA work. Barbara's goal for me had been to minimize the financial loss. Surprisingly, we generated a profit. And we found a new buyer for the event.

"You saved the day, Deb. Come back to New York with me," she said after the event. "This time, we'll watch the Virginia Slims women's pro tennis year-end championships. It's my thanks to you for directing our event. Such a big success! We set up a scholarship fund for junior tennis with the sale of our tournament. Kids will benefit for decades because of you. Love you!" She paused. "And bring Hadley."

At eight years old, Hadley was starting to compete in her own tournaments and was thrilled to join me. She enjoyed staying at the players' hotel in New York City, where she had an occasional brush with fame, like riding the elevator with a pro or sighting one in the lobby. Even Scott was impressed when he spotted Hadley on television in our courtside seats next to Barbara's dear friend Billie Jean King as we watched Monica Seles defeat Martina Navratilova in the final at Madison Square Garden.

Before the trip, we'd watched the newly released movie *Home Alone 2: Lost in New York*. Barbara suggested we recreate as many scenes as possible while visiting the Big Apple.

"What was your favorite part?" I asked Hadley on the flight home.

"My favorite part of the movie? Or of the trip?" she asked. "Well, I guess they're kind of the same thing."

She was right. We chased pigeons in Central Park, ate ice cream at the Plaza Hotel, shopped for toys at FAO Schwarz, and went ice-skating at Rockefeller Center—like in the movie. On top of that, we saw the Rockettes' *Christmas Spectacular* at Radio Music City Music Hall and *Secret Garden* on Broadway. Barbara knew how to treat us like princesses.

"I can't decide," Hadley responded. "It was all great! I'm glad you directed *our* tennis tournament, Mom," she said proudly, grateful to be part of the thank-you trip.

A month later, at Christmas, Barbara packed my entire family off to her beach house in Florida for a week. She was still thrilled about the tournament's success, but she also wanted to reward all of us for taking in Sergei and Lina while he awaited a work visa. Spending the holidays in a warm climate was a dream come true.

My family was fortunate to have been gifted these unique opportunities. Now, it was time for me to step up and deliver my kids a life filled with education, travel, and experiences. My prince couldn't provide what I wanted for them. Tyler would enter elementary school in a few months, and I needed to be a working mom on my terms—where I could earn enough while keeping the kids my top priority. And I wanted to find a permanent job that was as exciting as directing the tennis tournament had been.

CHAPTER 11

Going Global

*P*ocahontas had a secure life within her tribe and the affection of a solid guy. However, her curiosity, kindness, and courage opened opportunities and forced her to make a difficult decision about a new world that called to her.

After piecing together a series of part-time jobs, returning to work full-time meant rejoining the safe confines of corporate America. Eli Lilly had a position in line with my previous finance roles. Cummins offered something different, the role of international marketing manager. They saw my work on the WTA event and the beer distribution project in Moscow as sufficient experience in sports marketing and international business. From Dad's years at Cummins, I knew the company wanted leaders with a broad worldview. They also were known to mix things up professionally, like placing engineers in other functional areas such as HR. The interviewers at Cummins seemed to like my foundation in accounting and finance and how I'd layered on some global marketing experience. Lilly was the safe choice, but I jumped at the chance to pivot my career and explore marketing. It was much more fun! Cummins was willing to take a chance on me; shouldn't I decide to do the same?

"I feel like I'm going home!" I said.

"Your dad would've been proud to see his youngest daughter joining his longtime company," Scott said.

"If only I didn't have an hour-long commute each way," I lamented about the drive from our home on the north side of Indianapolis to the small Southern Indiana town of Columbus where I'd grown up.

My first big assignment was organizing a global conference with an agenda to address complex issues between the company and its distributors. Attendees would come from more than eighty countries. The weeklong event would take a year to plan, and the logistics would tax the infrastructure of our small town, where we'd host the one thousand attendees and their families. We only had one hotel with a single restaurant—and that restaurant was substandard. If I was going to rejoin corporate America, I wanted to do my best. That was the standard I'd held for myself as a student and in my prior positions. I was all in. We transformed the town to deliver world-class entertainment and found innovative ways to address topics and discuss strategy that week. Even the organizers from the World Economic Forum in Davos would've been impressed.

"J.I. Miller and his wife Xenia are coming to opening night of the conference!" I could hardly contain my excitement. He was a legendary figure, both in the company and in the American business landscape. "They agreed to do a receiving line. I hope they can stand long enough in this heat to shake hands with everyone," I said to a coworker, knowing I'd be the last one waiting in line. I'd admired Mr. Miller since I was a child, but we'd never met.

"For these global distributors, seeing him is like meeting the pope or Mother Teresa," my coworker commented, knowing how Mr. Miller's visionary leadership had opened the doors for Cummins's extensive global trade decades ago.

"You heard we got a photo with Mother Teresa and her Cummins generator?" I smiled, remembering our recent marketing coup.

"If you keep doing stuff like that, they'll have you running the whole marketing department before long," she said.

It was nice to receive positive reinforcement, but I was driven by an internal urge to do my best. I had a great team, and we delivered. I barely slept that week, leading to an emergency eye doctor visit on the event's last day. The diagnosis was corneal abrasions from wearing my contacts for too many hours. Even through my swollen eyes, I could see we had delivered a conference that would be discussed for decades. The leadership team was forever grateful and rewarded me with the first of many promotions.

The cultural fit at Cummins was perfect for me. At home, we struggled to help Sergei's daughter assimilate. I secured a scholarship for Lina at the Peter Rabbit Nursery School, but language was a barrier. She didn't speak a word of English when she arrived. She seemed afraid of everything and everyone. Her teeth were tinged pink from all the sugary Kool-Aid-type drinks she'd consumed in Russia, but no one knew because she didn't smile. Lina was also accustomed to sleeping in Sergei's bed, a practice we insisted needed to change now that she was five years old. There were two bedrooms upstairs, plenty of room, unlike their apartment in Russia. It was an excruciating process for her to adjust to the bedtime separation. My family endured Lina's nightly bloodcurdling screams for weeks.

It's a huge responsibility to adopt a family, and I couldn't do it alone, especially once I returned to work full-time. I implored my family to help. Hadley and Tyler took time to teach Lina English and shared their after-school babysitter with her. In addition to our home, we opened our hearts and took them on family vacations. Scott coached Lina's soccer team. Mom loaded them with birthday and Christmas presents. None of us imagined it would take so long to get Sergei established. Finally, after eight long and uncertain months, he secured a green card—the key to unlocking his future in the States and setting him on a path to citizenship.

As relieved as we were when Sergei got an apartment after living in our home for so long, the support didn't end there. He needed furniture, babysitting for Lina while he coached, and much more. The responsibility for supporting Sergei and his daughter was like raising children. I'd brought them into this (American) world and felt responsible for them.

While sharing our home had been hectic, the house felt empty without Sergei. He'd become a close friend and had been part of my life for the past three years. The experience with the Russians changed me. Without the tennis exchange, I would never have met Sergei or worked closely with Barbara, which led to the tournament director position. Without Sergei's help on the AB project, I wouldn't have been offered a fantastic international job and a bright future at Cummins.

My days were busy with the long commute, developing global marketing plans, picking up the kids from activities, making dinner, and overseeing homework. But after the kids went to bed, I had time to think. I missed the nightly chats with Sergei when everyone else was asleep. I appreciated how difficult it must be to start life over in a new country. He had many problems to solve, and I was still his chief problem solver—only now, it was mostly by phone: school forms to fill out, income taxes, health insurance, banking—an endless list.

Sometimes I'd head to Sergei's apartment after my kids were in bed to work through the challenges face-to-face. Scott was at our home (asleep at 8:00 p.m. as usual) but available for our kids. Marsha, Sergei's immigration attorney and a friend to both of us, frequently joined us. He was good at creating the image of a poor single father who needed help starting a life in a new world. Marsha and I were women who liked to support a good cause. Sergei was also a good host.

"Marsha, drink this Heineken," Sergei commanded.

"I never drank beer before I met Sergei," Marsha said. "But he doesn't take no for an answer."

"I know the feeling. I never ate ribs before. But you can't refuse the man," I said. "He convinces us to work for beer and barbeque. Should we expect the same payment from our next Russian 'client'?" I asked.

As a favor to Barbara, Marsha's firm donated her legal time to obtain Sergei's green card. But Marsha had counted on me to do most of the legwork rounding up letters of support, researching his education, and providing written translations. Barbara asked us to do the same for Valeria's son, a doctor who wanted to relocate to Indianapolis.

"Her son doesn't have any hard currency to pay but said he'd do *anything* to have my services." Marsha laughed.

"Marsha, Marsha, Marsha—he's married. To a Russian doctor," I said.

"I'm learning that Russians have different morals," she said. "And I'm good with that." She laughed again and winked at Sergei. "Another handsome Russian client to serve."

He looked up from the grill, smiling. He removed his shirt, and I stared at his broad, athletic shoulders.

"Gotta turn in soon; big soccer weekend starts tomorrow," I said, helping put the dishes away.

"Your kids are amazing, Deb. How many sports do they play?" Marsha asked.

"I've lost count. You can never have too many sports."

"You and Scott are the perfect Carmel parents—nothing but Indiana's best public schools and competitive sports for your kids. I, on the other hand, can sleep in tomorrow. No kids, no husband, just my cat. So, I'll stay awhile." She winked. "More Heineken, Sergei," she said, holding out her empty glass.

"Yes, ma'am!" said Sergei, eager to serve his guest.

When our life coaching and free legal services clinics wrapped up, Marsha and I usually left Sergei's apartment simultaneously. But tonight was different. When I got in my car, I hesitated and decided not to turn on the engine. I'd wait awhile, curious about how long Marsha would stay. I waited more than thirty minutes. What could be keeping her? Sergei wasn't much of a conversationalist with anyone but me. He was concerned with the quality of his English and was painfully shy around most Americans. Well, there had been that wink. But I was sure he could never be interested in Marsha.

Sergei wasn't mine, but he felt like family. So why was I still sitting there? This couldn't be jealousy. Sergei was my project.

He idolized me, and I highly respected his skills as an athlete and coach. Still, I didn't want another American woman taking my place with him. I started the engine. It was time to head home.

The next day, I told Scott about Barbara's latest request. "She wants me to help Marsha again by doing the non-legal legwork for Valeria's son," I explained. "I'm a pro-bono paralegal, I guess, specializing in O-1 work visas."

"A new Russian project," Scott remarked. "Just when you finished the last one."

Scott resented the time I spent helping the Russians. I resented his resentment. Why couldn't I hang out with friends sometimes and do something productive? He was no fun. I'd returned to full-time work to secure our kids' futures because he could not. I resented him for that. I didn't particularly like having such negative thoughts about Scott. God forbid I turn out like his mom!

Peggy had been mad when Scott's dad developed Parkinson's and had to retire early. She enjoyed being a doctor's wife with the financial rewards of that lifestyle. Peggy complained that their retirement funds would no longer be as large as planned. After the disease progressed, she acted embarrassed and made fun of her husband's struggle to walk. Scott and his siblings were saddened by how Peggy treated their dad. I suspected she contributed to the case of pneumonia that led to his death. He couldn't provide the kind of life she'd expected, so she resented him. It was horrifying to think that might now describe me!

"You're nothing like my mom," Scott often assured me.

I tried to analyze how Peggy had evolved. Life on the traditional princess path comes with high expectations. Learning your prince can no longer deliver the dream you imagined is a significant disappointment, but it doesn't permit you to become a monster. My approach was to solve the financial problem myself. I was no longer in love with Scott, but I refused to follow Peggy's lead.

My husband and I were still best friends and perfectly aligned co-parents. Yet ScottnDeb had become Scott and Deb. Scott frequently mentioned that he didn't want to live in an unhappy household as he'd experienced with his parents. So far, ours was a happy home filled with love for the kids. But what about when the kids were gone someday? What would my growing resentment for Scott's lack of ambition look like then? He deserved better than I could offer. Ever pragmatic, I wondered if it would be better to separate so we could hold on to the positives and not let things worsen over time. I think Scott had similar thoughts.

"I want to go to France, to Giverny to see Monet's water lilies . . . and to Roland-Garros. And I want to go to England for Wimbledon!" announced Hadley.

After my first year at Cummins, management rewarded me with a substantial bonus. I decided to start a new family tradition of taking each of my kids on a trip to Europe when they turned ten—a working mother–child adventure. Scott agreed. The child could choose the itinerary. Hadley was first up.

Forget the Fairy Tale and Find Your Happiness

"Maybe we can visit a castle when we're in England. And we have to go to the British Museum and the Tower of London to see the Crown Jewels." She had it all planned out.

Even on our mother-daughter European vacation, there was no escape from supporting the Russians. While Hadley stayed in Amsterdam with friends, I took a brief side trip to Moscow. I met Sergei's mom, Valentina, at the US embassy in Moscow with a letter I'd obtained from my congressman supporting her request for a visa to visit the US that summer. This was no easy task as Valentina had been denied for lying on her initial application. I untangled the mess as Sergei waited anxiously back in the States. We were rewarded with a favorable outcome: his mom got to visit—and babysit for Lina for the remainder of the summer.

"Amerikan vooman can do anything!" When he heard of my success, his admiring tone told me all I needed to know. Sergei and I had developed a special bond, and I never wanted to disappoint him. He had taken care of me in Russia, and I took the lead in the US. I liked my spot on the pedestal where he kept me.

In the beginning, Sergei reached into his stash of Russian art left from the exhibition years before and recycled pieces as gifts for birthdays and holidays. I built a collection of matryoshkas, ceramics, and Gzhel china. Shortly after the Europe trip, he gave me Krasnaya Moskva perfume from Moscow. The smell lingered and surrounded me.

"Vooman needs cologne. You can remember Moscow," he said.

Mom was the only other person who'd ever given me a fragrance. This was different. But he was right; I did think of Moscow when I wore the scent. And my time with him.

On the other hand, when I thought about India, I recalled the smell of curry. Cummins had wanted the board of directors to meet in India to witness their two joint ventures with Indian business partners. I organized the trip in partnership with the staff in India. We took seven aircraft and visited six cities across India during the monsoon season. We squeezed tourism around the plant tours and even had a visit with the prime minister. Before we started the planning, Cummins's CEO had challenged me to make India in the mid-'90s "feel like Disney World"—a tall task given the government red tape and lack of five-star tourism infrastructure.

"That's the Taj Mahal." Hadley pointed to the photo after one of my trips. "Did you see the mummy in the basement?"

"No, but Tyler would've liked the old-fashioned squat toilets available just outside the Taj," I said, remembering his tradition of checking out every bathroom wherever we traveled.

"Where's that museum?" Hadley wondered, pointing to another photo.

"That's actually a hotel room at the Taj Hotel in Bombay, overlooking the Indian Ocean," I explained. One room I'd stayed in was nearly as large as our home.

"My teacher says we're supposed to call it 'Mumbai' now," corrected Hadley.

"You're right! I keep forgetting. They changed the name this year. Look at this picture—behind the manufacturing plant, and you can see the foothills of the Himalayan Mountains."

"They have fireworks in India?" Tyler pointed to another photo.

"Yes. And since the Tata Cummins JV plant opening was on the Fourth of July, we added the fireworks."

Forget the Fairy Tale and Find Your Happiness

"No fair! You got to ride on a real elephant," Tyler complained, looking at another photo.

"My teacher says it's not nice to tame elephants," added Hadley.

"She's probably right. But the elephants didn't seem to mind," I rationalized this unintentional animal abuse. "It was difficult to get on and off. But when the elephant walked, it was like floating up and down on a fluffy cloud. Very different than riding a horse."

"I want to go to India!" Tyler exclaimed.

"I want a job in marketing, like Mom," said Hadley. For the time being, she settled on organizing an Indian-themed birthday party that year—inviting guests to dress in saris and sultans' hats as teams raced around town on a scavenger hunt.

I was learning so much at Cummins and was surrounded by examples of strong leaders who built on Mr. Miller's legacy of diversity and global growth. Marketing filled my need for a creative outlet—telling stories of how Cummins powered people's lives around the globe. It was a noble cause, and I loved participating in it. Fueled by the company leaders' belief in me, this feeling of confidence and independence was as powerful as the engines we were promoting. I began to write speeches for the CEO and put together the annual meeting and report. I'd even get to meet Paul Rand, the legendary graphic designer who had developed Cummins's logo and typically created the cover for the annual report.

My own vision was coming into focus, and I was beginning to find my path in the world. I began to picture a different life where I was not dependent upon a prince—a life where I could take care of myself and my family on my own. I was empowered to single-handedly deliver the financial means to fulfill my vision of excellent education and athletic opportunities for Hadley and Tyler.

Lesson 11—He Who Makes the Gold Makes the Rules

Somewhere during my eighteen years of required Sunday church attendance, I learned the Golden Rule: do unto others as you would have them do unto you. In my parents' home, we practiced an adaptation of that biblical admonition: he who makes the gold makes the rules. This meant Dad was the boss because he was the provider. Mom was a mere enforcer. Dad made all the big decisions—from family policies to major purchases like homes, cars, and boats. He also decided to pay for half of our college educations. Thank goodness for that one. I'm unsure how Mom would've voted on that issue for Teresa and me.

After Dad passed on from cancer, his gold continued to care for my mom, who was still in her fifties. Enhanced by a few investment decisions I'd made with his estate, Dad left Mom financially set for life. Scott's dad did the same for Peggy following his death, even if she complained that it wasn't as much as she'd expected. These women had never worked outside the home, but their princes secured their happily ever after—or at least their *financial* ever after. I think "happily ever after" and "financial ever after" were the same thing for them. I used to think I was entitled to the same type of princess path. Lately, I'd accepted that this fully financed golden years lifestyle would not be an option for me. Now that I was earning a significant portion of the family gold, the silver lining was that I could make some of my own rules.

One rule had been self-imposed since I first became interested in boys. I vowed never to date a guy shorter than me. That was a nonstarter. Granted, it became challenging when I grew to nearly six feet tall. But I needed to look up to my man—physically. When we met back in college, Scott met my minimum height requirements. But after nearly twenty years together, I realized he was now shorter than me, according to the yardstick. How did we get to this place? Did he shrink? Maybe it was all that running. Or did I grow? I *had* grown—in many ways, and I continued to grow.

I was no longer that college coed with stars in her eyes. Even though I hadn't planned to return to the workplace, I'd earned an MBA, become a CPA, run a pro tennis event, and led a project in a foreign country. Now, I managed a global team and sat at the table with the CEOs of major corporations. And all while being an involved mom of two bright children who understood there was a whole world for them to experience. I carried my height gracefully these days, no longer trying to slouch or avoid questions about what it was like to be tall. I enjoyed my elevated view. My vision became clear.

Scott was a fine man, but I needed someone to grow with me, someone with ambitions—not a guy who complained about his job for decades but never did anything about it. Neither Scott nor I wanted to become a bitter Peggy. It seemed better to cut our romantic losses short and remain friends for life.

I'd been married to society's concept of the traditional princess path with the man as the provider—the path my mom and most of my friends enjoyed. I felt entitled to that path. Every father figure I'd ever known wanted to provide for his family. But this wasn't only about money. I honestly believe I would have continued to respect Scott if he'd professionally pursued his passion as a runner or become a high school cross-country coach making less than an average engineer. Or if I'd been the wife who put her husband through medical school. We could've figured out the money if he had shown effort. But not caring about work was like not caring about us, which hurt. That was the part I couldn't understand and could not accept. Scott broke our social contract, and that was unforgivable to me.

The truth is, neither of us fought for our marriage. We sat by while it slipped away. I needed Scott to get on his white horse and fight for me. But sadly, he sat on the sidelines and watched as I invested more and more of myself and my time in Sergei, helping him to establish a life in America. I let society tell me that a prince was the provider and a woman's place was at home—unless she *wanted* a career. I considered myself progressive because I believed a woman had a right to choose anything, including her working status—yet I thought men did not. I was sexist because I resented Scott for low-key wanting to be a stay-at-home dad. I blamed Scott for not meeting my expectations for him, and I couldn't give myself to a man who could accept a path to the lower middle class if that's all that came easily. When that traditional princess path lifestyle became financially strained, I feared for my children's future, which shook me to the core. I felt completely responsible for them. I would make my own rules now.

We never took the kids aside and discussed Scott's move upstairs, which happened after Sergei and his daughter moved out. It was a natural move. I think we both believed we deserved a chance at something more. Scott agreed things couldn't continue like they had been. After a year of living on different floors, it was time to take the next step and end our marital illusion. The divorce process took months, but even after it was final, it would be many more months before Scott moved out and we began sharing our bombshell news with family and friends. Only Sergei knew. Like Scott, he was in my trusted inner circle and fully aware of our plans.

Scott and I carefully selected a neutral place to deliver our news to the kids—Carmel's City Plaza, where the rushing water of the fountains might soothe their tender souls as we gave them the information. The mandatory pre-divorce classes cautioned parents about where and how to tell their kids. Scott and I wanted to make the transition as smooth as possible for Hadley and Tyler, and, like everything, we would share the news together.

It was the most challenging message I ever had to deliver, and my stomach churned as we sat down at the picnic table. I wanted to protect our kids more than anything in the world, but I couldn't go on living a lie with Scott. It was time to tell them. I knew I'd have to be the one to say those first words: "You know how much Dad and I love both of you . . ." It gets hazy for me after that, but I'm sure the kids have vivid memories. After all, Hadley was eleven and Tyler was nearly nine.

Scott didn't move out until we could afford for him to move into a house around the corner. That was months after we'd told the kids. Our share of the profits from selling the condo in Moscow provided the funds for Scott's down payment. I didn't want him to move into an apartment and be alone. We looked at his nearby home as an annex to our family homestead. The long, drawn-out period between finalizing the divorce and Scott moving out gave us time to adjust. Above all else, Scott and I wanted to be the best co-parents and ensure a smooth transition for the kids. The divorce lawyer commented that it was the most amicable divorce she'd ever handled. But perhaps the delays in our communication signaled that we were ashamed to admit our failure as a couple. It was as if someone had died—ScottnDeb—and we couldn't discuss it. Scott and I never had one argument in seventeen years of marriage. Maybe we should have.

I was willing to sacrifice a marriage to hold on to my beliefs about a prince. The classic princess path had been my road map to a happily ever after but had led me to a romantic dead end. I needed to forget that fairy tale. Yet I knew Scott and I would continue to co-parent and the kids would be all right.

SECTION IV

Something There

In a tale as old as time, Belle eventually saw beauty in the Beast, a non-traditional prince. Ariel was willing to be a fish out of water for her man. Pocahontas was attracted to Captain John Smith, someone who was from outside of her community and who had different cultural norms. Jasmine refused to let society define her future; she wanted to follow her heart. Even though the guy was a street urchin, he was fun! Tiana transformed a lazy frog into a prince worthy of her love. Beginning in the '90s, the Disney princesses made their own decisions about the men in their lives. The characters had evolved.

CHAPTER 12

Prince Charming

Following her tribe's traditional path for women wasn't in the cards for Pocahontas. Grandmother Willow and the spirits advised her to let her heart guide her decisions. She needed to find her own path.

I'll never forget how it sounded. The *swish-swish* as our puffy coats touched. We faced each other and I leaned in, meeting his lips for the first time. My world shifted.

"What about . . . ?" he started. Then he kissed me back. Hard. I think he'd been waiting a long time for that kiss.

My divorce from Scott was not yet final when Sergei and I shared that kiss, but I wouldn't allow guilt to creep in. I was finally beginning to feel alive. I didn't want to risk losing myself again by following society's path for women. I still wanted a prince, but I wanted him for pleasure, for fun; I would no longer count on a guy to take care of me. I could take care of myself—and my kids. I thought Sergei might be that newly defined perfect prince. Who else? I would never date anyone from the office. The men at work were all married, and their wives viewed any working woman with a suspicious eye. I stayed in my lane as a blandly dressed, strictly business coworker and never gave the wives any reason to be jealous. I'd given up my tennis team, so I wouldn't find my prince there either. There was no time to meet anyone between my job and the kids. Sergei and I both had a sense of adventure and enjoyed lives inspired by tennis. I could see us owning a racquet club someday. We'd host tournaments and travel to all the Grand Slams, the Davis and Fed Cups, and Indian Wells. I could see it. And in our future lives, there would be no puffy coats.

Looking back, it's easy to recall that first kiss. But it had taken years to evolve my feelings for that shaggy-haired beast who didn't speak, smile, or even use deodorant when he first arrived in America. As his appearance changed, it became easier to see he was an entrepreneur filled with ambition, unleashed into a world of possibilities. Years later, Sergei was no longer a project who depended upon me for survival in America. He was fun and exciting—someone I enjoyed spending time with. My kids accepted him as a family friend. It took a long time for him to settle in America, but when he did, he became something more. Maybe it was a Pygmalion effect. I finally realized I'd fallen for my transplanted Russian project. Now, I saw him as an athletic and masculine Prince Charming who took my breath away.

The transformation had been mutual. Sergei brought out the best in me. I'd become a kind woman who opened her heart to immigrants. Sergei believed in me and encouraged me to dream big. Without him, I might still be an accountant in Indiana. Instead, an exciting new global path opened for me professionally.

Raised on Cinderella and Sleeping Beauty—blonde, blue-eyed girls who met a prince and lived happily ever after—I'd become disillusioned with that traditional princess path. While I was no longer a damsel waiting to be rescued, I still believed a prince was required for a happy ending. So, I adapted my belief. *This* time, I wanted to ride alongside my equally ambitious prince on white horses, seeking adventure. Both of us could slay dragons along our path to happily ever after. I had evolved.

"*Ya lyu-blyu vas*," I told Sergei—*I love you*. I was accepting my feelings and wanted him to know how I felt. The phrase I'd first learned from Barbara and later taught to Hadley's school class had a new meaning for me.

"Don't say that, Deb," he responded, not at all what I'd expected to hear. Had I misinterpreted his feelings for me? My stomach was suddenly sick.

"No. *Vas* is not the way. Man or woman say, '*Ya lyu-blyu tebya*,'" he corrected. "To say you love someone should be personal—*tebya* means 'for you.'"

"*Ya lyu-blyu tebya*," I said, wanting to be correct. My eyes searched his.

"Yes," he said with approval. But he didn't say it back.

Sergei was close to completing the five-year path to citizenship, enabled by his past tennis achievements, his immigration attorney's hard work, and my research and paperwork. At least I wouldn't have to worry if he was only with me so he could stay in America. If we ever did marry, it would be for love, not to gain his citizenship.

Mom had always been friendly with Sergei and his daughter, Lina. I didn't tell her about my divorce until Scott moved out about a year after the filing. When I finally did, she raised a concern.

"You know I'll always consider Scott as a son. But I knew something was off with your marriage for years," she said. "I hope you don't take up with Sergei now. I've noticed how he looks at you these days. Be careful with him; he has those *bedroom eyes*," she cautioned.

Lesson 12—Don't Trust a Man with Bedroom Eyes

As much as Mom liked watching movies starring Hollywood's leading men of her time, like Rock Hudson and Cary Grant, known for their masculine elegance and darkly handsome features, she was quick to point out that she'd never trust them. They were just eye candy. She said to watch out for men with smoldering, half-closed "bedroom eyes"—they were not the marrying kind. She described Clark Gable, Gregory Peck, and Robert Mitchum as "shifty ladies' men" with their come-hither looks. She warned us young girls to sense danger if a man winked or stared too long at us. Those men were trying to seduce us. "They want the milk without buying the cow," she advised. "Those kinds of men are for all women to admire—but not for one woman to marry. You must avoid choosing a handsome man for your Prince Charming." She paused. "That's why I never minded your dad's big ears."

I didn't inherit Dad's oversized ears, but after the divorce, I did feel like Dumbo, cast out and alone, around college friends and neighbors. I kept my private life separate at work, as I thought a working mother needed to do. There was no one to confide in about my feelings for Sergei. Even as people slowly learned about the breakup of ScottnDeb, I doubt they imagined I'd see anything romantic in my friend from Russia. I think they saw Sergei as my charity project or a tennis buddy. Unless they favored athletes, they typically described him as looking like "an unfriendly KGB agent." Although Sergei had developed a decent vocabulary, I could see why he might come across as a rude foreigner with his direct nature and broken English. I had no one with whom to share the thrill of new love or the red flags I'd noticed. And there were plenty of red flags. How do you tell people that you've recently discovered the guy you're interested in had *two* ex-wives?

"So, you'd be wife number three?" I imagined my family would reply.

"Well, you know three *is* my lucky number," I'd respond in jest. After all, my family knew I was born on January 3 at 3:00 p.m. "And by the way," I'd dare add, my imagination running wild, "I'd love to have another child—that would make three for me." But seriously, I *had* been thinking about having another child. I couldn't bear to think that part of my life was over. However, if Sergei and I *did* have a baby, it would also be his third. It was hard enough for me to accept that he had two ex-wives, but I'd also learned he had *another* daughter, one he rarely saw, who lived in Kaliningrad. He failed to mention his first wife and child for years.

Forget the Fairy Tale and Find Your Happiness

I definitely wouldn't share the details I'd learned about his first divorce. Sergei had cheated on his first wife with the woman who became his second wife. Nope. That would be too much information for my people. I wanted them to *like* Sergei, not gossip about him. I'd keep those red flags to myself, along with a conversation I'd had with Sergei during his green card application process years ago. That's when I discovered the timing of his *second* divorce.

"Sergei, the application needs the exact date of your divorce," I'd said.

"I don't remember."

"Well, here's a copy of the divorce decree you gave to Marsha. It's in Russian, but it looks like the date is July 1987. It must be a typo. Lina was born right about then. And in 1990, when you first came to the US, you told Barbara and all of us that you were married."

He was silent.

"You know you can't lie on these government forms," I'd said.

It turns out there was no typo. I learned that when Sergei's second wife was pregnant, he'd looked elsewhere for satisfaction and had an affair with a woman named Svetlana. His wife found out right after Lina's birth—and right after naming the new baby Svetlana. She promptly divorced Sergei and changed their daughter's name to Lina. When I asked how he'd reunited with Lina's mother, he said she took pity on him when he hurt his back and was hospitalized. I could see it; he was good at that. But she never agreed to remarry; they only lived together after that reunion. His mother-in-law never forgave Sergei and didn't speak to him even though she allowed her daughter's family, including Sergei, to live in her apartment. Andre wasn't a fan either—Sergei's stepson, whom I'd met at the Russian school years ago. No, I wouldn't be telling anyone that story either. And I wouldn't mention that Sergei had an older daughter, Nastia, who lived back in Russia with his first wife. That's another story I wouldn't tell.

The worst thing about Sergei, which I also didn't want to share with my people, was a situation I was involved in. I'd recently discovered that Lina's mother hadn't permitted him to take their daughter from Moscow to the States. This made me an unwitting accomplice by helping to obtain her passport and flight. Sergei was capable of both cheating *and* kidnapping!

How would people respond to learning that? No, Sergei was not the typical Prince Charming that you wrote home about. I wished I'd known all of this before I'd helped him bring Lina to America, let alone before falling in love with the idea of him—a tall, dark, exciting sportsman with a life in tennis. No, I felt I had to keep his relationship history to myself. No one would believe I could fall for someone like that, including me.

Life with Sergei was littered with red flags and red tape. I was sitting at the kitchen table, surrounded by a stack of Sergei's medical forms, when Scott came to the house to pick up Tyler one afternoon.

"Well, good thing you enjoy a challenge," Scott said, pointing to the pile of papers.

I think he was half joking. Even though we were no longer married, we still looked out for each other. I'm sure part of him was genuinely concerned that I would push myself too hard—at home or at work.

Scott continued, smiling. "First, his hemorrhoids were removed; then it was thyroid surgery. I wish we taxpayers had free medical care like you find for him. You even got IU's dental school to fix his rotten teeth. What's next on his medical agenda?"

I paused, squinting at Scott's outline against the glare of the afternoon sun shining through the sliding glass door. "I think his hernia," I replied, keeping the conversation within the humorous realm, although it *was* next on Sergei's long list of health-care issues he wanted to fix. "He's been lifting many heavy boxes lately—sending shipments to Russia."

Despite his talent at tennis, Sergei constantly tried to move away from his sports profession and instead make his living in "beeznuss" now that he was in America. Initially, he tried to sell goods *from* Russia to the US. Now, his get-rich-quick ideas were the reverse.

"Can you watch Lina while I go to Shoe Carnival?" Sergei asked for the third evening that week. I often provided her with after-school childcare, via my babysitter, even though they had an apartment a few miles away. They stayed for dinner almost every night too. Not to mention the business support I continued to provide. We were still a full-service operation in support of Sergei and his daughter Lina—that is, until he shipped over his oldest daughter, Nastia, to become his live-in babysitter.

"Yes, of course. But do you have buyers for all these shoes?" I asked. Sergei had been buying hundreds of pairs, boxing them, and shipping them to his friends in Russia for resale. He required constant help to fill out the various forms.

He winked. "Every Russian wants shoes. My friend will pay me back, don't worry."

Sergei had many friends who took advantage of him. They sincerely valued his friendship, even if they did take advantage of his generosity. He was a fun guy with seemingly endless exciting connections. Sergei had a big heart and was quite forgiving. His friend never reimbursed him for the shoe shipments, and I *did* worry—he barely had enough money to live on and was investing his small savings in this shoe "beeznuss." Because he lived in the US, his friends in Russia viewed him as wealthy and successful. The truth was, he struggled to earn a living, and without my family's support he probably wouldn't have survived in America. I thought he'd have a better chance if he stuck to tennis. This was his specialty.

"I'm sick of tennis," Sergei said. "You no understand how I hate it. These American kids so bad. No technique. No sportsmen. They don't want to be on the court; their parents want them there. These kids stupid. I make them run today. No tennis. Just run. Maybe they quit."

On the one hand, what he said was frequently true: tennis parents could be pushy, and many kids just went through the motions. But I had to respond the day he struck a kid with a tennis ball. "Sergei, you can't do stuff like that! You could lose your job!" I said.

"That kid stupid!" he replied with a vicious look in his eyes. Then he softened and drew me close. "I need you, *now*." Sergei didn't believe in foreplay.

My new Prince Charming had power over me. He "needed" me at unusual times and places, and I felt powerless to deny him. But while Sergei and I were a couple in private, we were rarely

Forget the Fairy Tale and Find Your Happiness

seen together in public. No kisses, no hand-holding. Scott had been dating a woman at his company for a while now, but none of us had met her. I assumed we were all uneasy with these new relationships and their potential impact on the kids. I wanted Hadley and Tyler to be comfortable. Co-parenting was going well with Scott. The kids continued to flourish at school and in sports. Sergei's youngest daughter idolized Hadley and Tyler. I pictured that we were becoming a beautiful, blended family like on *The Brady Bunch*, my favorite childhood show.

"Let's go bowling this weekend, Deb," Sergei said, picking me up in a bear hug before setting me on the kitchen counter. He relaxed his arms but held me close, nose to nose. "I going to beat you this time," he continued. His low voice was serious.

"Have you been practicing?" I asked.

He smiled, his eyes deeply creased. I frequently glimpsed his smile now that he had caps and was proud of his teeth. I wished he'd show this friendly side of himself to more Americans.

"You're worried I might beat you at a sport. Oh, wait," I added. "I beat you once at tennis in Russia, and I can water-ski better than you." His extreme masculinity, which was part of my attraction to him, couldn't accept losing to a girl. Ever the jock, it pained him that he could not master slalom waterskiing.

"Bowling is not a sport. And I gave you five games and thirty love that once in tennis. But yes, you are a *rusalka*—a mermaid on one ski. That's why I must marry you," he added.

Sergei began talking about marriage soon after Scott moved out. The divorce had been final for a year, but it was still too fast for me. My heart said yes, but I wanted to wait until there was more space for everyone.

While I felt like I understood this mysterious, brooding man's many layers, he was still full of surprises. After a long week at work, I found a bottle of champagne in the refrigerator. "What's this, Sergei?" I asked.

"*Shampanskoye!*" He smiled. "For my Amerikan vooman!"

Sergei never needed a reason to celebrate life. Bouquets frequently appeared on my pillowcase. A piece of jewelry would appear on the counter in my bathroom.

"Let's go snow ski tomorrow!" he'd say on a whim.

"I have to work," I'd respond, understanding how Scott must have felt in the past when I came up with fun ideas and he could only see his daily work obligations. But unlike Scott, I refused to become depressed at the limitations of a full-time job. "Well, I could take a vacation day on Monday when the kids are out of school."

"Amerikan vooman. I hope you do not ski as good on the snow as on the water!"

It felt natural to experience America with Sergei and the kids. I was so happy. Sergei had shown me the best side of his country. Beyond Moscow, he'd taken me to the canals and museums in St. Petersburg and waterskiing in Sochi. Years passed, but I never lost the desire to return the favor and always looked for opportunities to show off my country. Over the years, my family had taken him and his Russian visitors to places like Niagara Falls and Gatlinburg and to events like pro baseball games, NBA games, and the Indianapolis 500. We'd been to Hilton Head and back to Barbara's beach house in Florida. Along with the kids, Sergei and I shared a love of

Forget the Fairy Tale and Find Your Happiness

travel. This summer, I'd be taking Tyler on his ten-year-old trip to Europe, as I'd done with Hadley two years before. I booked an extra ticket for Lina. She was less than a year younger than Ty, and in anticipation of her joining the family, this would be a two-for-one way to include both kids. I also thought it would be fun for Tyler to have a friend along. He agreed.

I was a woman on the move. It was a busy and happy time between traveling for work and attending the kids' competitions on the weekends. For several months, I kept an American Airlines newsletter folded in my purse. It contained details of how to enter a contest for female travelers, and I filed the January 31 contest deadline in my head. *This* contest was not a mere lottery where the winner faced almost impossible odds. *This* contest rewarded customers' ideas. As head of global marketing communications for a Fortune 500 company, I recognized that I was that customer. I only had to find a few minutes in my busy life to type up and send a response. Finally, I sat at my computer and entered the airline's Female Business Traveler Contest for Women on the Move just as the clock was about to strike midnight on the deadline.

Two weeks later, I received a call at my office. A male voice greeted me with, "Happy Valentine's Day, Deb!" My mind tried to identify who this might be; it wasn't Sergei or Scott. The man laughed and said, "I love the reactions I'm getting. You are the fifth and final woman I've called today." By now, I was ready to hang up, but he introduced himself as the president of Wyndham Hotels, a partner with American Airlines in the travel contest.

He continued, "Wyndham is launching a Women on Their Way program. With our partner, American Airlines, we're flying you out for an all-expense-paid trip to New York City next week for some events and to meet with the press. You'll be staying at the Plaza Hotel. It's near some other venues, including the flagship store of Liz Claiborne, where you'll have a private fashion show and fittings as you take home an assortment of new fashions as part of your prize package. Of course, you'll also receive six round-trip flights from American and two weeks of vacation at any Wyndham Hotel you can use later with your family."

I hadn't noticed the list of prizes before I entered; I just knew this contest was meant for me. But how on earth would I be able to leave the kids and my job to go to New York next week?

Wyndham's president must've read my mind. He said, "I'm sure it will be tough to break away. You're the only mother, or working mother, for that matter, among the five winners. The other gals just work—and travel!"

I was the token mom. I'd made no secret of my status and used insights from my dual roles in my winning response. I'd described how my kids and I communicated while on the road and offered some tips. I'd talked about how faxes of my kids' artwork and graded papers lined my hotel room mirrors and how we practiced math by calculating the time differences to set up future phone calls. Now, all I could think of was how much I wanted to tell Hadley and Tyler that their mom had won a *non*-business trip, and I'd be staying at the Plaza Hotel, where they'd both been with Barbara and me in New York. The best part was that later, our family could enjoy the prizes of free flights and hotel stays together—wherever *we* wanted to go.

The kids were impressed when a stretch limo pulled up to take me to the airport. I truly felt like a princess. There were more limos in the city. The PR agency representatives took us to Cipriani's for a long dinner where the winners bonded

Forget the Fairy Tale and Find Your Happiness

over expensive wine (well, beer for me). The princess experience continued the next day at the Liz Claiborne store, which opened early for the five of us. After the private fashion show, we were taken to private dressing rooms where two to three personal shopping attendants (our fairy godmothers) took turns bringing us outfits they imagined would work on our various shapes and sizes.

Newly attired after hours of pampering, we floated back to the press event on cloud nine. The other four winners appeared nervous, but I looked forward to it. I'd been to countless press events—always coaching and prepping my CEO or other executives. Articles resulting from these interviews had appeared in top-tier newspapers from the *Wall Street Journal* to the *Financial Times*. I'd spoken to hundreds of analysts and journalists around the globe, but until that day, I had never been to a press event where I was the story's subject. Today, the press wanted to hear what I had to say—not my CEO. When the lights came on and the cameras rolled, the other girls seemed paralyzed and looked to me to respond. I relished every moment of that interview panel until the clock struck and the press conference was over. Then it was time to head home, back to a reality filled with work, chores, and kids.

My world shifted after that trip to New York. I began understanding what it felt like to be a professional princess—strong, independent, confident, and in charge. It wasn't just being a subject of the Women on Their Way campaign. I'd gone from being ScottnDeb to becoming the subject of my own life story. I didn't have to follow society's traditional path for women; I could listen to my head and heart and find my own way. And I could choose a non-traditional Prince Charming to join me.

CHAPTER 13

Hello, It's Me

Ursula explained to Ariel that there was no free lunch. Falling in love comes at a cost. It's not all shiny rings and champagne. You might lose your voice or worse.

Not everyone was as enamored with my new Prince Charming as I was. Financial constraints as a single mom meant that Hadley occasionally had free tennis hitting sessions with Sergei instead of eighty-dollar-an-hour lessons with the other club pros. "I know this is less than ideal, but I appreciate the cost savings," I told Hadley. I knew our Russian didn't offer the same positive reinforcement that Hadley enjoyed from her American coaches so she dreaded his sessions. She wasn't the only one. Tennis students often feared him, especially the teen girls—who coiled when he punished poor shot selection with push-ups. But Hadley understood the value of sparring. The summer's first big tennis tournament was next week, and she wanted to be ready. Hadley would qualify for the Midwestern Championships in Michigan in June if she did well at the upcoming event. She agreed to hit with him on Saturday.

Forget the Fairy Tale and Find Your Happiness

Hadley was Sergei's last lesson of the day, and I knew he'd be tired. I walked onto the high school court with her to smooth over the first few minutes of a hitting session between the two unwilling participants. Sergei didn't want to hit with Hadley even if the sparring sessions improved her game. He was mentally tired of the sport and preferred to spend time resting or working on his business schemes. He especially disliked non-paying clients like us. Sergei's previous student, a lady from one of his women's clinics, was still on court, slowly packing up.

"It's too hot for tennis," he complained, his comment probably directed at me.

His adult student handed him her water bottle. "Here, Sergei." Then she reached for a towel and gently gave it to him, her hand lingering after he accepted it.

A few weeks later, Sergei flagged me down at the same high school courts when I dropped off Hadley one summer morning for her daylong group lessons. He leaned in my driver's side window and asked me to swing by his apartment, pick up the lunch he'd left behind, and bring it to him. That added an extra fifteen minutes before starting my long work commute. But I knew he depended on me to help him out.

I opened the apartment door with the key he'd given me a few months earlier and noticed the blinking flash of the answering machine. I thought the message might be important, like a lesson time change or someone from Russia with an urgent request. He often asked me to listen to his messages from Americans to help him fully understand their meaning. I didn't think twice about hitting the "play" button to jot down a note.

"Sergei, it's Betsy. I keep thinking about our drive to Chicago this weekend, taking your oldest daughter to O'Hare. Thank you for letting me get to know her. My brother called. He's looking forward to meeting you and Lina on Friday. He knows how serious we are and wants to meet the man in my life. I already miss you, and it has only been a few hours. Love you."

I froze. Faced with the reality that the man I thought I would marry was seeing another woman behind my back, I could see that any hope for a happily ever after was finished with one voice message. Even though I was running late for work, I decided to confront him.

"Who the hell is Betsy?" I demanded, throwing his lunch bag at him. He'd excused himself from his group lesson when he saw me arrive. We stood by the parking lot, just out of earshot of the hundreds of students, including Hadley, and dozens of coaches.

"You met her before, over there," he said, motioning to the court where Hadley and I had met his adult student a few weeks earlier.

My first thought was that this woman was not his type. I'd met his second ex-wife, and she was ultra-feminine. With short hair and glasses, *this* woman looked like a masculine librarian. She had large calf muscles and played tennis in a running jersey and shorts.

"You asked me to marry you!" I said incredulously. "Did you ask her too? What kind of a man are you?"

"You never want to marry me," he said softly, blaming me for his actions.

"That is not true, and you know it. We were becoming a family! We just took all the kids to Mammoth Cave!" I tried to reconcile why he would say this. Yes, it had taken eight months for my ex-husband to move out, but that was a while ago. Last week, *he* wanted to look at rings!

"I love you, Deb. She mean nothing to me," Sergei said, trying a new tactic.

I wanted none of it. "I never want to see you again. And I'm not taking Lina to Europe in July." It occurred to me at that moment that he'd probably planned a vacation with that woman while I was babysitting his daughter in Europe. No. More. I was sick of handling everything in his life for him. "We are finished!" I roared. "That's it." I didn't care who overheard me at the tennis courts. *I* needed to hear it.

I drove on to work but could not focus on anything. The next day, I called in sick for the first time ever. My heart wasn't the only organ suffering. My bowels had turned to liquid, leaving me weak in bed. I kept the shade pulled and put the pieces together. I realized he'd been making the phone calls I'd received over the past few months where someone called, heard my voice, and then hung up. They weren't just creepy; they were to confirm that I was home. He must have been going out with her and wanted to ensure I wasn't nearby! These small moments haunted me. I had to see the truth to believe it—or, in this case, hear it. I kept replaying Betsy's voicemail in my head.

In bed, I experienced wild hallucinations. I imagined lying to Sergei and telling him I was pregnant so he'd have to stay with me. I couldn't believe a man could do this to me. This is not what Prince Charming does! We'd talked about marriage; I only wanted more time! Scott and I had taken over a year to inform people about our divorce. This meant Sergei and I had not been open about our relationship until recently. I thought

Sergei shared my concern about showing respect for Scott and not being publicly seen as the new happy couple. But maybe he just wanted to appear single—not dating anyone, including a divorcée like me. I panicked. Without Sergei, I would be a divorcée for the rest of my life. And I'd never have another child! Life was over, and I was still in my thirties! I had another wild thought, and this time I acted on it.

"Scott, do you think we might ever get back together?" I asked my ex-husband by phone. By now, he'd been dating a woman from work for quite a while.

"Yes. But not if it was like before," he responded.

I think he meant our lack of sexual relations. But he also could have been referring to spending all my energy on the kids, serving Barbara, and helping immigrants—especially Sergei and all his friends and family. And I always threw myself into my work. The bottom line was that I hadn't invested in our relationship for a long time. I can't say he did either. No, Scott was right. We could never get back to the way we were in the beginning. That traditional path hadn't worked, the one where I thought he'd provide for us as my dad had done. I'd already accepted that the way forward was to forget that fairy tale.

I felt so stupid. How could I have fallen for a cheater? I knew what real love looked like—I'd had it with Scott in college. I settled into a cycle of feeling stupid, being mad at Sergei, and getting sad about my future. I'd begun to think about having another child with Sergei. Now, I'd never be a new mom ever again. In six months, I'd be forty. Stupid, mad, sad. Rinse and repeat.

The questions about that woman continued to torture me. When did Sergei start this relationship? How did they meet?

I decided to ask her myself. Besides, I'd want to know about the other woman if I were her. She was probably like me, a naive Midwesterner, but she was also a victim. She needed to be warned. I got her number from the tennis club and placed the call.

"Deb," Betsy said. "I heard you confronted Sergei about me at the courts the same day I learned about you. We gave the tennis staff *two* entertaining shows about his infidelity that day." She sounded amused when I called her, not crushed like me.

"Did he tell you anything about us?" I dared to ask.

"He told me that he loved me—that you didn't mean anything to him," she answered.

"That's the same thing he told me."

We both agreed that he was a two-timing jerk. Betsy and I endured several painful but enlightening conversations, and I began piecing it together. I had to make some sense of it. These calls were therapeutic yet left me drained.

"My neighbor's daughter is one of his star junior students," Betsy told me. "The mom wanted to fix us up. She saw us as two eligible singles in our thirties—a good match."

No tennis pun intended, I thought. But somehow, I liked this woman. She was nice. We could've been friends under different circumstances.

"My neighbor encouraged me to take his adult women's tennis clinic on Thursday nights so we could meet. She told me he was a single father who needed a mother for his young child. I learned he had two daughters and that his older daughter had come from Russia to help watch the younger one while he was coaching. I felt sorry for him," Betsy said.

I recalled how Sergei often went out "with a group" after those evening tennis clinics. Sergei's oldest daughter, Nastia, had visited that semester, supposedly to attend school and learn English. It had been a considerable effort for me to help get her settled, but her arrival also meant my kids no longer had to share their after-school babysitter. But I felt terrible for Nastia. Now that Sergei finally had an opportunity to get to know her, he seemed more interested in her skills as an unpaid cook and babysitter. She was an eighth grader, only a couple of years older than Hadley. But her presence in their apartment as babysitter meant Sergei was free to roam whenever he liked. Betsy repeated what I'd heard in that voice message: he told her he loved her when the two of them drove Nastia to the airport for her recent return to her mom in Russia.

Both Betsy and I initially rejected Sergei. After a few weeks, however, Betsy fell back under his spell. "Hello, Deb," she said when I answered her call. "I wanted you to know that I've decided to work through things with him. After all, he wasn't married to you, so technically, he didn't cheat on me," Betsy rationalized.

I was glad she was honest with me about her intentions. But should I mention to her that Sergei continued to try to reconcile with me? Should I play *those* recent voice messages for her? No, I figured she knew enough about his character by this time. The calls with Betsy ended. My trauma from wondering if it was her every time the phone rang began to subside. I started the slow process of rebuilding my life.

Tennis helped. While I'd dropped out of my league years ago, watching Hadley play tennis was a good substitute for my competitive nature, and lately it helped take my mind off things.

Forget the Fairy Tale and Find Your Happiness

She qualified for the big Midwest tennis event, and together with Tyler, we spent a glorious week in Okemos, Michigan, with the other qualifiers from Indiana and their families. Kids developed character out on those hot summer courts in hard-fought matches. At night, there were fun Ping-Pong matches by the hotel pool while the parents drank cold beer.

"Remember, Hadley, it's Tyler's trip to Europe this time, so he gets to make the decisions. But I'm glad it worked out for you to come along." We'd been able to change the tickets from Lina's name to Hadley's.

"Me too," said Hadley.

"Me three," added Tyler. "And I want to visit as many countries as possible, unlike Hadley, who only visited England, France, and the Netherlands on her ten-year-old trip."

With the aid of Eurail passes, Tyler's itinerary packed in eight countries over two weeks. While my heart still ached about Sergei, I couldn't have asked for two better companions on the road. The time away and the busy schedule helped to ease the pain.

I was grateful to have a tremendous job and two incredible kids, even though I'd surrendered two princes and perhaps any chance for romantic happiness. I hated to admit it, but maybe Mom had been right about Sergei. I shouldn't have trusted him with my heart. My brother, Tom, thought all Russians were Communists and had never approved of my associations with them. I rarely saw my sister, Teresa, anymore. No, my family would have no sympathy for Sergei's departure from my life. And ScottnDeb had stopped hanging out with mutual friends after splitting. I could've used some friends that summer but didn't have any since I was no longer part of a couple.

I never discussed my personal life at work either. This was part of my belief that women at work must be generic and not act feminine. No gossip. Just the facts. This approach served me well as I advanced quickly through the ranks to become a "woman on her way." As far as people at work knew, I was still married to Scott even though we'd been divorced for about eighteen months. After the divorce, I'd removed my thin wedding band but still wore my engagement ring to avoid questions. I didn't feel single yet; I felt isolated. But I wasn't alone—I had my kids.

The phone rang one Sunday morning in late summer. I'd avoided the phone for months, since the Betsy fiasco, letting everything go to voicemail. I didn't want to speak to him—I couldn't. I wasn't strong enough. I wondered how I'd summoned the courage months ago to confront him about the cheating the last time I saw him.

I knew it was over, but I sensed that Sergei still held some power over me. When we were just friends, I'd dedicated myself to helping him, especially after he moved to America. Over time, I became attracted to him. Lately, I felt like I had to stay away from him entirely or I might not be strong enough to turn him away—like a person with an addiction. I'd successfully avoided him at the tennis courts when dropping off or picking up Hadley. I could see who was calling when the phone rang if I ran to the fax machine at home or looked at the caller ID on my office phone or car phone. But after a long

Forget the Fairy Tale and Find Your Happiness

summer in isolation capped off by our incredible European vacation, I felt stronger. Today, I felt confident enough to pick up the phone and speak with whoever was on the other end.

"Hello, Deb," he said in a soft, hurt voice, desperate to connect.

"Uh-huh." Why did I pick up the phone? *Remember, you're strong enough*, I told myself.

"Lina misses you so much. And your kids. And I miss you."

I remembered the cheating and how sick I felt—the stupid/mad/sad cycle. Then I thought about how much stronger I was now thanks to my hard-earned progress over the long summer. Still, the sound of his voice took my breath away. I didn't want it to, but it did.

"What do you need, Sergei?" I assumed he had a transactional request. Maybe he had a new medical issue, or needed something related to his upcoming citizenship application, or wanted some information for a business deal he was working on. I'd spent years of my life helping the man.

"We want to see you today, your family. We miss you," he pleaded.

Hadley was out of town at a soccer event with Scott and the travel team. Tyler and I had planned to go canoeing at Eagle Creek Reservoir that afternoon. My mind flooded with thoughts. I wasn't sure I was strong enough to resist his potential advances. His sad, pleading eyes. His intoxicating deep voice. Then I wondered if Tyler and I were strong enough to paddle around the lake on our own. Maybe it was wise to have another adult in the canoe. Sergei was so strong. And I felt bad for Lina. She didn't get to go to Europe with us. No doubt she would have a lonely day sitting around their apartment. He never took her anywhere on his own. Hadley said that without access to our babysitter, Sergei had dumped her at the tennis courts all summer. But Lina wasn't my responsibility. Could I ever forgive him? He couldn't just walk back in!

"How's your girlfriend?" I asked. I figured I might as well go right to it.

"I don't see her anymore. You know that. You know everything," he said, implying I was somehow up to speed on his love life. I wasn't. After those calls with Betsy, I'd spent the summer trying to forget.

"So, you've missed out on another potential mom for Lina. I'm sure you'll find another," I said, letting my hurt turn to meanness.

"Don't. Don't, Deb. This woman don't mean anything to me," he said.

I realized I was the one who'd brought her up, and frankly, I didn't want to hear anything about her. At that point, I only wanted to go canoeing.

"Lina can go," I found myself saying, knowing it would mean a lot to her.

"She happy to go . . . Can I go too?" he maneuvered.

An hour later, I positioned Tyler in my car's front seat to avoid direct contact with Sergei, who was seated in the back. It was a beautiful day on the lake. He took his shirt off in the canoe, and I could see his strong, broad shoulders as he single-handedly paddled us around. I felt safe and could relax, unusual for a single parent. It was almost like old times when we were just friends—before Sergei and I became romantically involved and before his cheating. Perhaps we could just be friends again, he and I.

His physical advances started only a few days after our canoeing expedition. "You never even said you were sorry for what you did," I said, pushing back in protest. Why had I thought he'd go along with just being friends?

"I'm sorry! So sorry!" he said, still trying to wrap his arms around me. "We weren't married. You not want marry me," he claimed in his best broken English.

"That's not true." I tried to counter his explanation, which relied on his alternative reality. It *wasn't* true, but I did accept *some* responsibility for his wandering since I'd been slow to tell the world about my divorce from Scott. Yet his relationship with Betsy was the biggest red flag since the previous deception about his two wives, divorces, and children. I wasn't ready to talk about marriage again, but he was relentless, and after two weeks of courting/harassing me, he worked his way back into my heart and bed right before he left on an extended trip to Russia. Maybe our love was meant to be.

"Do you promise there will be no other women, period? In America or while you are in Russia, Sergei? I don't want you to forget that is the deal."

"I don't want you to forget about me," he said. He "needed" me frequently in those few days between our reconciliation and his departure.

Always searching for the next big deal, Sergei wrapped up his summer coaching job at Barbara's club, sublet his apartment, and left for Russia. I agreed to take care of Lina so she could continue school. She was thrilled to be back with my kids and me.

After he was gone, I learned from Barbara that the club hadn't renewed Sergei's employment. She commented, "Sergei couldn't keep his pants zipped," referring to his summer romance with Betsy. I didn't dare to share the part about our prior or recently revived connection.

"Hello, do you miss me?" Sergei said when he called me from Russia. "Lina said you are going to London. You need to come to Moscow!"

Sergei had been away for about six weeks when I received a last-minute invitation to speak at a conference in London. A matter had come up recently, and I wanted to discuss it with him face-to-face. This was probably my best chance to do that since he seemed to be in no hurry to return to America. I agreed to fly from London to Moscow for the weekend before heading home after the conference. I barely had time to change my ticket and get the three kids squared away with Scott and the babysitter. Then I swung by Walgreens for the second time that week on my way to the airport.

Sergei was staying with Victor, the actor, but reserved a hotel room for my stay. "I knew you'd come." He was happy to see me, more pleased than I'd ever seen him. Once in the hotel room, he held me in what can be described as a Russian bear hug. He locked his arms around me with bone-crushing strength while lifting me off the ground.

Barely breathing after his release, I noticed he couldn't stop smiling. He usually didn't wear emotions on his face. "Is there time for me to shower before dinner?" I asked. It was high on my to-do list after attending the conference all day and then flying across Europe. I was surprised when he pulled back the curtain and stepped into the shower to join me. The shabby hotel "shower" was an old freestanding, cast-iron, claw-foot tub. And it was small. I wasn't sure there was enough space for two people to stand, but he squeezed in anyway. And that's where I received his official marriage proposal.

"I've been thinking here in Russia. Thinking about you. You are my vooman, and I want to marry you. You are the only one who understand me. Tell me, Deb, yes, that we can be married." He spoke in his lovely baritone voice.

I guess that's why he'd been smiling so much. After all the drama from the summer breakup, my response would typically be a hard no. But this proposal came at an interesting time. It was my turn to share a surprise.

"Sergei, I think we're pregnant." I could hardly believe it myself after the infertility issues Scott and I had suffered. We'd used condoms when we'd been together before he left for Russia, so it felt like a miracle. This was meant to be.

"A baby! No. Yes? Are you sure?" he sputtered with surprise but happiness.

I thought he might question this, so I'd brought another pregnancy test. I had taken one before I left for London because my period was a few weeks late. I wanted to rule it out because I figured I'd have some beer on the trip. When I saw the results, I couldn't believe it. I thought it was God telling me I needed to marry Sergei. There was some powerful, universal force at work between us. A greater purpose that had brought us together across continents and cultures. Past my divorce, his lies, and our breakup. It was an everlasting love, like in *Doctor Zhivago*. But to be sure, I'd bought another test kit on the way to the airport.

"Let's do the test now, and we can both see." I stepped out of the shower.

"Pink," I reported after the requisite wait. By now, we were dressed.

"Does that mean we have a girl?" he asked nervously.

"It means we are pregnant. We won't know what it is for a while."

"We *are* getting married!" He was thrilled.

The moment I was pregnant, I knew I would marry him. There was no other way. This child would need a father.

Lesson 13—Every Child Needs a Father

Mom had forbidden my sister and me to smoke, drink, or cuss, and we also knew where she stood on unwed mothers and their children. "The first requirement," she explained, "is for a girl to be a virgin. Next, she must get married in the eyes of God. Then, when a child comes, everyone will know it's legitimate. And no one can tease the child." She added, "Girls must stay away from married men as they mess up the whole system."

I believed she spoke from personal experience about her own mom, but I didn't dare ask and doubted she'd answer truthfully if I did. Mom would go to her grave with that one. But my theory would explain the whole *Mama Eva moved to Michigan from Georgia when Mom was a toddler and raised her as a single mother during the Great Depression* scenario. Dad's situation was only slightly better. Mama Dell was married when

Dad was born, but her husband disappeared early on, and Dad didn't have a father until Mama Dell remarried years later. So, neither of my parents had a father growing up. Mom made us promise never to do that to a child.

"Every child needs a father," she said. "Even a scoundrel is better than nothing."

It was all happening so fast. First, I got a marriage proposal from Sergei, and then I shared my news about the baby. I was still absorbing his initial reaction when he stuffed a wad of money into the top pocket of my denim shirt. "For the ring," he said, adding, "get a nice one."

Later, I counted two thousand dollars. For someone who hated to carry more than twenty dollars at a time, maybe one hundred dollars when traveling, holding this amount made me nervous. Would I need to report it to customs? What if it was lost or stolen? Once safely home, I relaxed and added three thousand of my own funds. I wanted a nice ring too. This was okay to do under my new definition of a prince as a partner—not a provider. Further breaking tradition, I walked into the jewelry store and picked out my ring while Sergei remained in Russia for a few more weeks. The clock was ticking. *Don't worry, Mom, there will be no bastards.*

A few weeks after the proposal, as I watched Hadley play in a local tennis tournament, I felt something unusual and went to the bathroom. My fear was realized; I was spotting. I called my OB, and she said we should meet immediately at her office. After her examination, she told me I'd lost the baby. I would need a D&C. Her office was next to the hospital. I was crushed, and there was no chance to call Sergei. He was still in Russia. I was alone.

I awoke from the general anesthesia in the hospital's recovery room. I have always hated hospitals, except for the two times I'd left with beautiful babies. I'd lost my baby this time, and I had no husband. It was unbearably cold in that room. Then I realized this was the hospital where my sister Teresa worked—in the recovery room. Oh my God. Yes, that was her over there. Even in my semi-conscious state, I was worried about what she would think of my situation. Would she tell Mom? This was a disaster. I'd lost my baby. Sergei's baby. Our baby. The nurse told me I could be dismissed soon, but someone else would have to drive me home. I couldn't ask Teresa. The only one who would understand was Scott. After returning from Moscow, I'd already told him about the pregnancy and impending nuptials. He came to the hospital right away to drive me home. A day or two later, Teresa did call me. She'd seen my chart and knew I'd been to the hospital. So much for the new HIPAA rules that had been enacted the previous month. At least she cared enough to call and check on me. I hadn't seen her in a year.

Even though the pregnancy had been unplanned, I did want a child with Sergei. Losing a child made me realize how much. Hadley was twelve, and when I thought about her going away to college, something inside me panicked. I loved being a mom and going through life with my children. They were my joy in life, and I worked hard to secure their future. I didn't want the raising children part of my life to be over. I also believed Sergei and I had a love that existed across continents and through the Iron Curtain. It would be beautiful if our union produced a child; our love would live through that child. I knew the birth would be a marvelous experience for Sergei as he hadn't witnessed the arrival of his two daughters. In the former Soviet Union, dads were never allowed in maternity hospitals, let alone the delivery room. They stood on the street below, waving flowers for about a week until mom and baby were released. And he wanted a son.

I reasoned that it made sense to go ahead with the wedding. I loved the man, and we had been separated and survived. I loved being a mom, and at thirty-nine years old, this was my only chance. I didn't want another borderline unwed mother scenario to explain to my sister or mom. That would also be a poor example for my children, even though they had accepted Sergei as part of our family for years. Sergei had rented out his apartment before he left for Russia, and I didn't want the kids to see us share a bedroom until we were wed. That was taboo in our society. The only thing to do was get married when he returned to America.

"Where do you want to have the wedding?" I asked. I hadn't been to church except for holidays in years, and it didn't seem right to have a church wedding for a second marriage.

"On court, of course," he answered.

A few days later, a justice of the peace performed our ceremony on tennis court #9, near where we'd first met years ago. Lina was disappointed to learn her last name wouldn't become Miller, like my kids. She, Hadley, and I had our hair styled together earlier that day. I wore an off-white crepe two-piece outfit trimmed in lace. Hadley got cold feet at the last minute. She'd resented Sergei ever since the unfortunate situation with

Betsy. Being a student in the tennis program and enduring all the gossip about him had to be embarrassing. And she had to deal with his meanness on court. Hadley refused to watch the ceremony and sat in the van in her fancy clothes and updo. Tyler stayed with her in a show of solidarity. But our newly formed party of five did go to a Japanese hibachi restaurant afterward to celebrate. *Kanpai!*

CHAPTER 14

Russian Hotel

Hardworking and ambitious, Tiana learned that kissing a frog prince was no shortcut to a happily ever after. There can be severe consequences. The way forward became a tough slog through a murky swamp. What a royal mess.

Days after we exchanged our vows on a tennis court, I heard the fax machine chugging and walked over to check it out. "Sergei, this is a flight itinerary for Nastia." I read on. "Who is landing here on Saturday? Did you forget to tell me you'd invited her to visit?" I asked, thinking this was a rude surprise.

"It's my daughter. She going to live here," he stated with authority. Nastia had struggled the last time she'd been in America, given that she didn't speak English. Nastia had made it clear that she missed her mom and didn't like living in America or being used as child labor for a half sister she'd never met until coming to this country. Now, she'd be in high school. There had always been tension between father and daughter—daily screaming fights, but those had taken place in their apartment. If Sergei couldn't manage her, how could I?

"What do you mean, to *live* here?" Daughter or not, I didn't feel like he had the authority to add her to our international Brady Bunch without at least talking to me about it. I was sensitive to Hadley's and Tyler's feelings and recognized that we must assimilate our new family carefully. They had opened their home to Lina for months (again) while Sergei was away in Russia, and we'd made that adjustment. We'd just started adding him to the mix. Adding Nastia right away would be a lot to absorb. I had flashbacks to all the times Sergei had filled our home with unannounced Russian guests who had stayed for weeks and expected the red-carpet treatment on my nickel. I felt like we were reopening what Scott had called the Russian Hotel. The differences in how we viewed our home/hotel illustrated our cultural divide.

"She my daughter," he repeated rudely, raising his voice and stating what seemed evident to him: he did not need to ask permission.

"Husbands and wives have to communicate with each other or it doesn't work, Sergei." I stated what I thought was obvious. Nastia had not been part of the daily life I imagined.

I got a call a few days later from the orthodontist. Sergei had taken Lina to Hadley's orthodontist and added her charges to my account. They informed him that my insurance would cover about half the total cost; his response was to bill the rest to me.

"Sergei, did you start your daughter with Dr. Barbour?" I asked when I got home from work that day.

"She need the braces," he mumbled.

"Well, insurance doesn't cover everything. You'll need to pay the down payment and then more later," I explained. "The office said you told them to put it on my credit card."

"I don't have money," he said, as if that explained why he felt he could charge a couple thousand to me, especially without first asking.

"I don't have this in the budget!" Although I had a good job, I also had a lot of expenses, and an unplanned expense for braces would be a setback. It was another major communication breakdown, and we were only about a week into the marriage. "When do you start coaching?"

Now that he was back, getting a new job seemed like it should be a top priority. He could approach many clubs in town despite losing his last job. "I am not going to coach anymore. I going to have car beeznuss."

This was shaping up to be a disastrous start to the marriage. I thought I had married a tennis coach! I knew his income was limited, but at least he'd had *some* income. This car business sounded like another Russian wild-goose chase, like shoes and caviar.

Our "honeymoon" came a few weeks later. It was a family trip to Arizona at Christmas, where Hadley played in her first national tennis tournament. We used the first of two free weeks from the contest I'd won and stayed at a Wyndham hotel in Phoenix—all six of us piled into one room. Sergei elected to sleep on the floor curled up with Lina, or "Linochka," as he fondly called her. He left his wedding ring at home because it "bothered his hand on the racquet."

On January 1, we returned from Arizona and another guest checked into our Russian hotel. Victor, Sergei's friend, arrived unannounced for an extended vacation. We'd only been married a month, but the partnership with my charming new prince was already on the rocks.

A lot can happen in a month. Because of my recent miscarriage, we were supposed to wait six months to get pregnant per the OB. Given the rough start to the marriage, that sounded like an excellent idea. But soon after we returned from Arizona, I learned I was pregnant. Again.

"You need abortion," Sergei said, looking straight ahead as he drove. "It's not a good time for me." That was his only explanation. "Just get it done."

"I will not!" In disbelief, and equally horrified at how routine it seemed to him, I turned to the car window to hide my tears. He'd wanted the last baby—the one I announced at the Russian hotel in Moscow. What had happened in the previous few months, except that we were married this time? I had an overwhelming feeling that I would be raising this child alone.

After a few days, Sergei accepted that I was proceeding with the pregnancy, and once Victor, our long-term guest, heard the news, Sergei swung into celebration mode. A sonogram was scheduled for a few weeks later. I was a high-risk pregnancy, given I'd just turned forty and had a recent miscarriage. Sergei was amazed at the possibility of seeing the baby with a sonogram. He planned to meet me at the doctor's office.

Before I could leave my office for the appointment, I got a surprise phone call. "Is this Deb?" a familiar voice asked.

I felt sick. It was Betsy.

"The tennis club gave me your number," she said, echoing how I'd tracked her down in odd symmetry less than a year ago.

I stood to close the door to my office so no one would hear this call. I didn't want to listen to it either. Betsy's voice terrified me.

She continued, "I figured you'd want to know Sergei visited me today at work. He was with a friend from Russia." She paused. "He introduced me as his girlfriend..."

Victor was in on this too. I had to remind myself to breathe.

"I'd heard at tennis that you two were married, and I didn't think this was right—his visit."

"Was he... Did you get the impression he was trying to..." I couldn't find the words.

"It was clear he was trying to restart our relationship." Betsy finished my sentence for me, confirming my fear. "*I made it clear I was not interested. I didn't feel comfortable having him at my workplace. It was kind of creepy.*"

I got the picture, and it wasn't good. But it was worse than even Betsy could imagine.

"I'm pregnant, Betsy," I confessed.

"Oh, Deb, I'm so sorry for you," she confided. "I have to tell you. Last summer, after you broke up with Sergei and he and I got back together, I sometimes thought *you* were the lucky one because you were strong and broke completely free from him. He can't be trusted; we both know that. I was surprised to hear you'd taken him back."

I wasn't feeling lucky. I called Sergei and left a voicemail about Betsy's call. It wasn't surprising that he failed to show up for the sonogram. Sergei and Victor didn't check into our Russian hotel that night. They were AWOL. I was in shock. I drank a few sips of wine to calm myself down that evening after the kids went to bed. I rarely drank wine, and I'd never had any alcohol during my previous pregnancies. I hoped neither the shock nor the wine would bother the baby. I vowed there would be no more wine. I had to take care of my baby—alone.

I had always trusted Scott completely during our seventeen years of marriage, and I always would. Even still, our marriage failed. But Sergei had already proven himself to be untrustworthy. Does a marriage without trust have a chance? Once my antennae were up, I couldn't put them back in. Everything fell under suspicion. I wondered about other women. Every woman. Did they think I was stupid for staying with him? Did *they* sleep with him? I especially wondered about Russian women; many had different value systems than Midwestern girls, at least the Russian women Sergei introduced to me. I learned that affairs were not uncommon among Russians. Men felt entitled to relationships outside of marriage. If a man kept it secret, other Russian men admired him, and he was considered clever. But my value system relied on fidelity and trust.

How could our life together move forward? But I'd been taught a husband was necessary for a pregnant woman. So, I'd have to fix this. Fix him. I wondered if he needed more sex than I'd been willing to offer. I couldn't get rid of that voice in my head, wondering what I'd done wrong. The stupid/mad/sad cycle started up again.

Sergei claimed Betsy was crazy, and Victor backed him up. I tried to put it out of my head, but soon after, I found a woman's business card in his coat pocket. Taking a page from the Betsy dialogues, I called the woman. It turns out this *was* strictly professional. It was his probation officer! He would be required to see her monthly for the following year.

"This was related to his shoplifting arrest," she explained.

What!?! While Sergei was dating Betsy the previous summer, he'd tried to slip some beef ribs out of the store in his shopping cart without paying. He wanted to impress her by making his famous barbeque. I was married to a man with a record. How would this affect his quest for citizenship?

I had no previous experience arguing with people. But that's all Sergei and I seemed to do. I had to speak up and speak out to him. Loud was the only language he could understand. We didn't just argue about the big things—we argued about *everything*. I asked him not to touch our laundry because he shrunk everything, mixed colors, and otherwise ruined anything he touched. He didn't care to learn how to do laundry properly, and yet he wouldn't stop washing clothes despite our pleas to leave it to us. Along with my patience, our wardrobes were also shrinking—in size.

One thing that wasn't shrinking was my job. Cummins remembered I had a finance background and liked how I'd marketed the company to customers in our international business. Leadership wanted me to market the corporation to the media, the financial community, and employee stakeholders, so they promoted me to director of investor relations and public relations. However, I didn't want to return to finance since I'd been so happy with marketing. I shared that with them, and I also shared that I was pregnant. They said for me to work my magic in this new role until the baby arrived, and then they'd let me return to marketing in an expanded corporate role when I returned from maternity leave. I agreed. But talking to financial analysts proved to be about as stressful as communicating with Sergei.

With four kids, one on the way, and a challenging new job, I needed a vacation. We used the six airline tickets I'd won in the contest to fly to Jamaica for spring break and stayed for free at a beautiful Wyndham hotel. Four months pregnant, I still scaled the boulders up the beautiful but harrowing Ocho Rios waterfall to keep an eye on my daredevil, Tyler. Hadley and Nastia were both capable of climbing on their own. Sergei carried his Linochka, but I didn't trust him to look out for Ty. Since Nastia's arrival, Sergei had drawn a definite line between his children and mine. My kids were second-class to him, including the new baby. Sergei couldn't have cared less for his pregnant wife and unborn child on our perilous hike. He only had eyes for Lina. Tyler and I survived the rocky climb. Instead of apologizing for leaving us to navigate the dangerous terrain, Sergei was angry we'd taken so long. Then there was another delay; we needed to stop for gas on the drive back to the hotel.

Sergei stepped out of our tiny Jamaican rental car at the gas station. He and Nastia exchanged angry words in Russian while he filled the tank. Sergei disappeared into the gas station store, emerged with a Red Stripe beer, and stood drinking near the car's hood. He leaned forward with one foot on the bumper and glared at us. His menacing look told me this situation would not end well. The tank was full, but he made no motion to replace the pump and get into the car. I got out, paid for the gas, put the pump back, and tried to reason with him.

"I'm sure Nastia didn't mean anything," I said, guessing. They constantly bickered about nothing.

"You always take their side!" he shouted, gulping more beer.

There was no reasoning with him when he got like this. I would've left him there, but he held the keys, dangling them before us. I got out of the car again and offered to drive, although I was worried about driving a stick-shift car on narrow mountain roads on the opposite side of the road than I was accustomed to. He scoffed and bought more beer.

Lesson 14—Manuals Are for Men

When I was growing up, there were different departments in my home. Dad handled the DIY projects. As an engineer, the first step he took was to read the manual before putting something together, although I don't think he ever needed instructions. Mom never opened a manual, but like a good secretary, she filed all of them in a drawer in the laundry room in case Dad needed to refer to them later. We probably had decades' worth of appliance manuals stashed in the cabinets.

Mom avoided another kind of manual. Dad preferred to drive a stick shift, which is how Mom described cars with manual transmissions. She refused to learn, declaring that "manuals are only for men." No, those manuals definitely didn't fall into Mom's department either. She was strictly an automatic. Me too.

Over an hour passed at the Jamaican gas station and darkness set in. The kids, who had been angry with Sergei at first, were now scared. The five of us were still seated in the hot car, afraid to be left behind if he made a sudden move. I discussed the situation with them, and we all agreed I should ask the station attendant to call the police for help. The police arrived and spoke sternly with him. They handed me the keys and told me he could not drive due to the drinking; either we could take him with us or they would take him to their station. I let him decide. He grudgingly stumbled into the passenger seat of our car, slamming the door. You could almost see the steam coming out of his nostrils as he stared straight ahead.

No words were spoken on the slow but harrowing drive back to the hotel. Somehow, we made it, and so did the gears of the rental car, which survived my jerky shifting skills. This was a defining moment. A line had been drawn between Sergei and the rest of us, the four kids plus me. There was no "his and mine" that day. We all saw his temper, and they knew I would do anything to keep them all safe, even manage to drive a manual transmission. The five of us completely ignored him and enjoyed the rest of spring break. We found that a free week at a Jamaican hotel on the beach can be fun and relaxing, even with no alcohol, six people in a room, and a brooding Russian man sitting in the corner by himself.

I was headed to a Saturday OB appointment at the five-month mark of my pregnancy. I discovered that the main door to the office complex was closed on weekends and took a shortcut through the overgrown lawn to reach another entrance. My foot fell into an unseen gopher-sized hole in the tall grass, and I collapsed from the pain. I'd turned my bad ankle again. I'd hurt it a year before, and it had never quite healed. But this was excruciating pain. The car was about twenty-five yards away, and crawling was the only way. I learned what it meant to see stars. Everything was flashing white. All I knew was to drive home somehow. It was challenging between the stars and pain and using only my left foot. At least the car was an automatic.

Of course, Sergei was in Russia for a few weeks, so Scott took me to the ER. The baby was fine, but the doctor determined I'd broken a bone in my foot and torn ligaments. I asked if I could travel to London the following day, where I was to meet Cummins's CEO and CFO for investor meetings. They'd left to golf in Scotland a day earlier, and I had all the meeting materials packed in my bags. The doctor said the baby was good to go, and the cast would stabilize the injury. I'd be mobile with crutches. My company counted on me to deliver, and I was the sole breadwinner. I would not let the company or my kids down.

A flight attendant ordered a cart to greet me upon landing at Heathrow and take me to a taxi. When the cart driver learned I had a broken foot and was pregnant, he volunteered to take me all the way to the airport hotel where I was staying that night. On that trip, I gained a new appreciation for the challenges disabled people faced. I also gained a new appreciation for those who offered assistance. As I struggled with the steps leading up to my five-star London hotel the next day, I realized nothing was handicap-friendly in this town. Each curb or step felt like a mountain to climb. The crutches didn't work well with a growing baby belly, but I somehow managed. The two days of meetings were successful, and top management was pleased.

The trip home was miserable. I developed a sinus infection, and the pain in my sinuses brought tears on the takeoffs and landings. One flight attendant noticed and leaned in to offer some comfort. My cast was visible, but it wasn't obvious I was sick or pregnant at that stage. Kindness from strangers can be such a powerful force. It was still daylight when I reached home and collapsed in bed, but I couldn't sleep; the sound of construction outside kept me awake. I'd received a bonus earlier that year and decided to build a swimming pool. It was a lifelong dream; I thought it would be a good investment for all the kids.

About seven months into my pregnancy, I pulled into the driveway after a long week at work. The long daily drives were becoming incredibly uncomfortable, and I looked forward to stepping into the new pool and floating all weekend. But I couldn't pull into the garage as a car blocked the way. I called Sergei on the car phone I'd received from Cummins.

"Friends here from Moscow. We drinking beer by the pool. Come over!" He happily invited me to my own home.

"How long are your friends planning to stay?" I asked, not revealing that I was in the driveway and not pleased to hear news of more freeloaders when all I needed was rest.

"They stay one month. We have a lot of beeznuss to talk about." He confirmed my worst fear—our hotel was still in business.

After spending a month at our home, another of his tennis buddies/business friends had recently left. In addition to Nastia, there had been a steady stream of guests since our marriage. The guests always spoke only in Russian, and Sergei did not try translating or interacting with my kids or me in English. Lina could no longer speak Russian, so she was also left out of their conversations.

    I backed up the car and left. I couldn't take it anymore. I needed an American hotel, but there were none close by. I was tired of working long hours and paying for their meals and entertainment while they enjoyed a vacation around my home and now the new pool.

    Since marrying me last fall, Sergei had never looked for work. He just invited guests to come and stay and explore business ideas. If I challenged him, it led to arguments. At night, I needed some sleep to climb another mountain the next day—at work and with the kids. To avoid conflict, I began sleeping on the floor of our walk-in closet, quite uncomfortable in my pregnant state. I resented Sergei for keeping the bed and letting his pregnant wife suffer on the floor.

    He'd see me curled up on the floor and jeer his standard line: "You have a problem? I don't have any problem." Then he'd return to the bed and drift peacefully to sleep.

    But that night, I knew I could not sleep at home, not even on the closet floor. I wasn't sure where to go for peace; I was too tired to even go somewhere for food. I found myself driving to Scott's nearby home. Scott had remarried months after I did, and I knew he and his wife were out of town with Hadley and Tyler at a soccer tournament. I'd never been in their house but knew where Scott kept a spare key for the kids. I never asked or told anyone, but I stayed in their guest bedroom that night. Without any supper, I just collapsed and slept like a baby.

    The following morning, I made the bed and went home without leaving a trace. I approached the Russian delegation poolside and demanded the guests check out immediately. My kids would be home soon, and my baby was on the way. It was all too much to ask of me, of us. My appearance and demands surprised Sergei, but his group left within the hour.

Even without the pressure of hosting outside guests, the cultural divide within our home continued. Our house had two sets of rules, and it wasn't working. I held my kids to high standards in the classroom and set boundaries, curfews, and expectations. In contrast, Sergei gave Nastia no guidelines. While he wanted her to perform better in school, his solution was to verbally abuse her when she received poor grades and then yell at me if I suggested setting study hours. She'd made some friends, but those kids smoked and drank, and most were failing school. This was unimaginable for ninth graders, and I knew this situation had to be resolved. The last straw was when Hadley and Tyler questioned why they had to study since Nastia didn't. I valued my children more than life itself, and I could not allow an up-close bad example to ruin their futures.

My strong nesting instinct was also kicking in, and I was concerned about preparing a nursery for our new baby. This would likely require moving Nastia out of Tyler's former nursery, but Sergei refused to discuss this possibility. He thought the baby would stay in our room for a few years. This was unimaginable to me. Nastia was homesick for Russia and her mom, and she badly wanted out of our American Brady Bunch. It would be a win-win if Sergei would let her return to Russia. Eventually, without a word, he booked a ticket to Russia for her a few weeks before the baby arrived.

A dark cloud lifted when Nastia left, along with her constant Russian shouting arguments with Sergei. There hadn't been any Russian guests since I'd put my foot down. I was off the closet floor and sleeping in my own bed. The cultural divide diminished. There was only one vacancy left to fill. That spot was being held for a tiny new permanent resident. I was about to fall in love all over again.

CHAPTER 15

Three's a Charm and Four's an Alarm

When they began their fantastic journey, Anastasia and Dimitri were strangers from different worlds. After all, she was raised as a princess and he was a con artist. She never imagined the adventures they'd have together or the love that would develop. Family had always been Anastasia's happily ever after. Was it possible to blend two worlds? If you can't have it all, what choice would you make?

Three weeks before my due date meant only one more week to make the uncomfortable 120-mile round trip to work with an unborn child sitting on my lap. I planned to host a Chinese delegation those last few days and then begin my maternity leave. There'd be plenty of time to get ready for the baby. After all, Hadley and Tyler both arrived late. It was a cool September Saturday night, and I was standing in the bedroom, carefully ironing the fabric cover for the baby's first scrapbook, like the ones I'd prepared for Hadley and Tyler. I figured one more spritz of steam and some pressure with the iron ought to do it. I leaned in with my arm and body.

"Sergei!" I called out when I felt warm water trickle down my leg. He was watching television just down the hallway. I waddled into the bathroom. My water had broken, a first for me. With the two previous births, the doctor had pierced the bulging sac. Sergei didn't respond to my initial call.

"Sergei!" I pounded on the wall of the shower stall. This time, he came running but stopped when he saw the bloody mess.

"What's happening?" He looked panicked.

"Call the doctor and ask if we should go to the hospital or wait," I said.

He ran to locate my mobile phone and then shoved it at me. "You call!"

My hands were wet as I punched the number on the speed dial. Calling seemed like a task he should handle, but this was no time to argue, so the call took place in the bloody shower stall. The doctor instructed me to head straight to the hospital. At least Sergei drove.

I thought I'd figured out all the possibilities with a third delivery, but no. Like Tyler, the baby was breech. Since my water had broken this time, the doctor only briefly attempted to turn the baby (that was the good news) before calling for an emergency C-section (and there's the bad). Throughout the pregnancy, I'd imagined that Sergei would enjoy watching a birth for the first time. Instead, he witnessed an operation—at least until the part when he fainted in the operating room.

Mom came to be with the kids for the never-long-enough hospital stay insurance covers after a birth. Mom was anxious to be released upon our return from the hospital, and after pausing to coo over the new baby, she left. Moments later, Sergei announced *he* was also leaving. He had car beeznuss in New York, he said. And just like that, he left me alone after emergency surgery to care for an infant and three children.

I could barely walk to the door when the bell rang later that week. "Hi, Barbara. Nice to see you. Come in."

"Where's Sergei? It's a time for pampering! Stay in your pajamas and let others bring meals and the baby to you," she said. "Especially after surgery."

"He'll be back in about a week, but the kids are a big help," I said. "What a beautiful baby blanket. How did you get Ally's name on it so quickly?"

"Oh, I had someone make it. I wasn't sure if you wanted her full name, Alexandra, or her nickname. Hope you like it! We wanted to give a warm welcome to your little one."

"It's perfect, Barbara. Thank you."

"Anastasia would've been another good name for your princess. That children's movie is going to be released soon. How will the producers handle the tragic ending if it's based on the Romanov royal family?"

I could not escape the Russians. They were in my home and on the big screen. I wondered if my life was evolving in parallel with an animated princess. Probably not this time—Anastasia didn't have a big job, a house full of kids, and a new princess to single-handedly care for. But there would be no tragic ending to this story. My kids would all have a happy ever after; I'd see to that.

Baby Ally was a child of the world. Not only were her parents from two different countries, but her first trip outside the US was at age seven weeks when Sergei and I took her to Cancun, Mexico. A few weeks later, her nanny arrived, an au pair from Brazil. Unlike with the arrival of my first two children, I needed to return to full-time work shortly after giving birth. I still wanted Ally to have one-on-one care even if I couldn't provide it during the daytime, so a carpenter built a suite over the garage for our nanny. Ally was only twelve weeks old when my maternity leave ended—and on the first day back, I boarded a plane for China. Ally was left in the care of the nanny, my mom, and Sergei. Hadley was learning to pitch in. There was a village to manage the baby and relieve my overall mother's guilt during that brief overseas absence.

We introduced Ally to tennis at an early age. She dozed in my arms in the stands as we watched Hadley's practices and tournaments. Ally took her first cross-country trip when the family drove to Atlanta and watched the Russian tennis team play in the Davis Cup at Stone Mountain versus a US team that featured Andre Agassi and Jim Courier. An eighteen-year-old Marat Safin was playing; he was much taller than he was when he stayed in Indianapolis at age nine. We hung out with the Russian coaches, who were Sergei's friends. Marat almost pulled out the win for the Russians, and we could see he was on his way to great things.

The car business hadn't taken off after a year and a half, so when one of Sergei's tennis buddies arrived from Russia, they decided to coach together. In the past, Rishat had checked into our home for a month. When I learned he intended to stay for six months this time to complete some requirements for a used car shipment, I put my foot down. I'd learned my lesson about the Russian Hotel stress on the family and me. Since then, we'd added a baby and a live-in au pair. My answer was no.

I thought Rishat would return to Russia after a few weeks and we could get on with our lives. After all, he had a baby boy back home about the same age as Ally and a tennis club to manage in a suburb of Moscow. He'd left his wife alone. But instead, Sergei chose to move out of our home and got an apartment with Rishat. My husband left me! He chose a friend over our family. This was devastating news to me. Sergei took ten-year-old Lina with him, although he still planned to drop her off at my home daily for babysitting. I didn't want to punish her for his decision, so I stayed silent. I was not her mom, but I *was* a stable figure in her life. Since Ally's birth, Lina had asked about her mom as she couldn't remember her. She often asked me if she looked like her mom and wanted me to tell her things about her mom even though I'd barely known her.

The shock of Sergei moving out was right up there with the discovery of Betsy's voicemail. But this time, I couldn't afford to spend a day in bed feeling sorry for myself or take a summer to figure things out. I left the next day to take Hadley, Tyler, and young Ally to Hadley's annual Midwest tennis championships. The kids loved this event. They had good memories of Michigan and the hotel stays with the other Indiana families.

My husband hurt me by deserting his wife and infant daughter. I wanted to return the favor. I had just a few hours to react before the tennis trip. I knew the man and figured he would come back to the house while I was gone, making himself at home. Sergei liked to impress his friends with the fringe benefits of a breadwinning American wife. Sergei and

Forget the Fairy Tale and Find Your Happiness

his friend would lounge around the pool and hot tub, clear out my refrigerator, and maybe host a Russian party. Furious at this thought, I decided to change the locks. He could either be in or out of this family, and he'd chosen to be out. I placed the things he hadn't relocated to his temporary apartment in bags on the front porch. There was no need to enter the home in our absence. We left for Michigan.

Ally took her first steps at that event. It was quite early, as she had just turned nine months old, but she was already a wiry little athlete. Hadley—the proud big sister—and her friends doted over Ally. Many of the same tennis families attended the major junior tennis events that summer: Clay Court Nationals in Boca Raton, Hard Court Nationals in Atlanta, and Team Zonals in Asheville, North Carolina. At each national junior tennis stop, we watched Ally's progress from those first steps in Michigan to walking to running. Sergei missed all of it.

Most importantly, with Sergei and Lina gone, order and calm were restored in our home. There was none of his shouting—just three happy kids and one hardworking mom. We benefited greatly from our second au pair, who arrived from the Canary Islands to replace our original Brazilian au pair when she left a few months early in pursuit of an American husband. We stayed at Barbara's beautiful home in Florida during Hadley's clay court event. It was a glorious summer. I had struggled to forget Sergei two years earlier after learning about his other woman. This time, I didn't mourn the loss. I knew how tempestuous life was with him as a husband, and I quickly learned that it was much more peaceful without him.

Rishat left after six months. Without any discussion, Sergei moved his things back into our home one day while I was at work. The au pair couldn't stop him. He acted as if nothing had happened. But for me, something had changed. Russian matryoshka nesting dolls reveal a smaller doll each time they're opened. Similarly, my love for Sergei had grown smaller and smaller each time he hurt me or I uncovered a new lie. We'd enjoyed the respite without him. I learned I was strong enough to survive—without a husband. I *could* do it on my own. I should thank him for that.

I allowed him to return because we shared a child, and school was starting for Lina. I explained that his return would only be possible with specific ground rules. There would be no Russian hotel at our house except for pre-approved visits on agreed-upon dates. Sergei was also required to begin contributing to monthly expenses. He had not done so in the first two years of our marriage while living for free, pursuing his car business, coaching tennis, and pocketing his profits. Sergei agreed but refused to continue coaching tennis and switched to truck driving as a new source of income. He'd heard about this occupation from other Russian immigrants and thought he could continue his used car sales business with Russia by phone on long drives. He was gone much of the time, which meant peace in the home.

I came home one evening, relieved our au pair, and spent time with Ally. I called out to the three kids to ask if they'd already had dinner. Hadley and Tyler were upstairs in their rooms studying and answered that they had each eaten independently after they came home from sports—which was the usual process. We were long past a sit-down family dinner since each person had a different daily schedule. One family member was in charge of the meal each day. The au pair pitched in as needed. The system worked well for us, and the kids learned to cook. Today was Hadley's assigned day, and she'd made Hamburger Helper. I confirmed with Lina that she had also eaten. She was entertaining herself in her bedroom on the first floor. After I put Ally to bed, I went into the kitchen to get something to eat. Sergei arrived from his truck driving job and stormed by, not acknowledging me as I sat at the kitchen table eating a late supper. I could tell by his glare it would be one of those nights when he would shout about something. Too bad. The silence had been so peaceful when I got home. Even the television was off. In a few minutes, he was back in the kitchen.

"Why my daughter eat dinner by herself? Nobody eat with her," he bellowed in a threatening voice.

"Sergei, none of these kids get here simultaneously; they often eat alone. This is not new," I tried to explain. He was rarely around at dinnertime on school nights. At first, I figured he'd just had a bad day.

"She's crying in her room. She said nobody ate dinner with her. She eat by herself." Now he was getting that scary look in his eyes—the violent look I'd last seen in Jamaica.

I'd already spoken with Lina, and she was completely fine. She could, however, be an actress for him. She would dip her head and bat her eyelashes at him—her Linochka look. She'd speak to him in a falsetto voice to achieve her goal. I knew my kids and his daughter—probably much better than he did. Hadley read a book at the table during meals if no one objected. Tyler would gulp down his food and be gone in a flash to return to a video game waiting on pause. Neither cared who else was at the table but would never exclude anyone.

Lina, on the other hand, craved attention. She was neither athletic nor academic but would talk anyone's ear off about sweet nothings. Typically, Lina talked nonstop at the au pair or me as we watched Ally. She would usually eat with our au pair if I wasn't home. Eating alone might feel like torture to an extrovert like his daughter, but this was no crime.

"Sergei, she's eleven years old and can eat by herself sometimes. If she's sad, it probably has nothing to do with dinner. She keeps asking about her mom lately. Maybe that's it. Do you want me to go talk to her?" From where I sat in the kitchen, I had a full view of the great room, and I saw Lina standing by the fax machine, listening to our conversation. When I looked over at her, she scampered down the hall toward her bedroom. *Busted*, I thought.

Out of nowhere, he lunged at me from across the room with his fist clenched, screaming in Russian. When I rose from the table, he pinned my back against the sliding glass door, his fist an inch from my nose.

"*Ya ub yoo tebya!*" he shouted, threatening my life.

"Get away from her or I'll call the police!" Hadley yelled from upstairs. She stood at the railing in the loft with a clear view of the scene below. Hadley didn't understand much Russian but recognized this situation was dangerous for her mom.

Sergei immediately backed away, mumbled something derogatory in Russian, and stormed out of the house. Hadley rushed down the stairs and hugged me. Tyler too. Hadley, only fourteen years old, had acted bravely. Lina emerged and was crying now. She realized her silly complaint about eating alone had sparked this attack and apologized. But it wasn't her fault. It was *his* fist in my face. I knew what I had to do.

Lesson 15—If He Shows You a Fist, Show Him the Door

"Where's my *real* grandfather, Mom? Dad's *real* dad, the one with the same name."

"He died a long time ago," she replied. Everyone was pretty tight-lipped about this part of our family history. But I figured Mom was more likely to talk about Dad's side of the family than he was.

I pressed for details. Kids need to know where they're from. "How did he die?"

"I think he was gassed in World War I and later died, or maybe it was TB. I'm not sure; Dad doesn't like to talk about it," she said.

"So, he was a war hero!"

"No, I don't think it was anything like that," she said, changing the subject.

I decided to ask Mama Dell about this the next time I saw her. She always answered my questions. I could ask her anything.

"What happened to my real grandfather in World War I?"

"I'm not sure. That was before I knew him," Mama Dell replied.

"Well, did he get any medals of honor or help to change the world or something?"

"No, I'd say the war probably changed him. And over time, it got worse for him. We divorced when your dad was pretty young."

"Mom said *you* left him. She said you took Dad and left," I said. I didn't think moms ever left dads, just the other way around.

"If a man gives you a reason to go, you need to go. Don't ever forget that," she said.

"What reason did he give to you? It must've been a good one."

"Little Deb, he showed me his fist. That was reason enough. When a man does that, you show him the door, or you go out that door yourself. And take the children with you."

That night, I called Marsha, the immigration attorney, and she recommended a family law practitioner. I temporarily locked Sergei out with interior locks, but this wasn't a sustainable solution. Recalling the Peking Hotel in Moscow, I knew he could chop down a door if he wanted to get in badly enough. I met the divorce attorney the following day.

"Have you filed a police report yet?" the attorney asked. "This is the first step to establish a record of abuse."

I was taken aback. This was serious! Combined with his prior arrest for shoplifting, I thought he'd never have a chance for citizenship, and I wasn't sure I could do that to him or Lina. I didn't believe he would ever hurt the children. He also was aware of Scott's ongoing presence. Scott lived nearby and visited most days, despite having a young daughter from his second marriage.

The current problem was different from our relationship's other ups and downs; unlike when Sergei cheated, refused to contribute financially, and constantly invited unannounced long-term guests into our home, there were safety concerns now. I was finally ready for a divorce and paid the attorney to prepare the papers. When the first draft arrived, I read the conditions. The one about custody was unacceptable. The lawyer explained that we would have to divide Ally's time. I would have to release Ally to him for a sizable chunk of her childhood. This was a showstopper.

I'd seen how he raised his other daughters, and I never wanted him to be alone with Ally for any length of time. His parenting skills were nonexistent. He'd deserted Nastia and later used her for cooking, cleaning, and babysitting. He'd kidnapped Lina when Sergei asked me to help them come to America. I felt terrible about this for Lina's mother, although he claimed she didn't want her daughter. I told myself this mother must envision her daughter having a better life in America so she had not complained. Maybe I'd been wrong about that.

Would he kidnap a child again, this time *my* daughter, and take her to Russia? The thought terrorized me. He could not be trusted with Ally at any level until she was old enough to protect herself. I was stuck. The only way to keep her safe was to stay married to him. I figured he would eventually move back to Russia. He struggled to make a living in the States, and it cost relatively little to survive in Russia. I resolved that I would have to make things work until he left or until she was eighteen years old. I couldn't discuss it with anyone other than the lawyer without risking tipping Sergei off. I knew he didn't want the responsibility of raising Ally, but he would exploit the situation for personal gain if he understood the stakes. That much was certain.

So, I took him back again. However, the issue of having two family value systems under one roof remained. We would never be the blended Brady Bunch family I'd initially envisioned.

"Get in the car! You are going to tennis," Sergei shouted at Lina.

"No, I don't want to go with you. You're mean to me on the court. I hate tennis," she cried out, lunging to the floor and grabbing my ankles as I stood at the stove in the kitchen.

"Sergei, you can't force a child to play a sport if they don't want to," I said, horrified, bending down to comfort the child, who was holding on for dear life.

Through her tears, Lina mumbled something about wishing he would drive his truck away and leave us alone.

"You, *you* are the problem," he said, shaking his finger at me. It was better than a fist but still unsettling. "Tell her she needs to go with me. She only listen to you."

"She and I listen to each other. We communicate," I replied. "You should try it sometimes instead of shoving or shouting at her. No wonder she doesn't want to be on a court with you. Sports are supposed to be fun. This child is telling you that playing tennis with you is not fun." I bent down to comfort the sobbing mess at my feet.

"Tennis not supposed to be fun!" he said, storming out.

Sergei seemed jealous that Lina aligned with my kids and me. And he *was* jealous when he compared her report cards to theirs. But instead of encouraging her, Sergei screamed at her . . . and me. In the past, he'd focused much of his negative energy on Nastia. With her back in Russia, and under the stipulation that he contribute to the family income, Sergei took out his frustrations on the rest of us. When he wasn't yelling at Lina, he babied her—his little Linochka. There was no middle ground.

Forget the Fairy Tale and Find Your Happiness

Lina begged me to ask Sergei if she could meet her mom in Russia. I figured these questions were normal. But raising the subject further enraged him. It seemed he didn't want to test the full custody he'd stolen years ago. I thought this issue was probably best settled between him and his second wife. My job was to give Lina a stable and inclusive home with clear guidelines and a good school district. I asked the au pair to devote even more attention to overseeing Lina's homework process. I dedicated time to helping her with spelling every week; Hadley and Tyler pitched in on other subjects. It was a team effort, except for Sergei. He only rolled his eyes because there was little progress despite all the hand-holding. Lina wasn't a natural student; she never had been and likely never would be.

Sergei decided Lina needed to learn to speak Russian as a future job skill—but he was too lazy to teach her. He stopped shouting long enough to hear her plea to meet her mom, whom she hadn't seen since she was five. He agreed to let Lina fly alone to Russia to be with her mom and attend school there the following semester.

Lina's absence made it peaceful again at home, even with Sergei there. There was one family value system. Our au pair focused on young Ally for once instead of being monopolized by Lina. Sergei began spending some time with Ally. The three of us took a trip to Hawaii. I thought he would notice how smoothly things were going. When Lina left, Sergei stopped contributing to the family funds, but it was worth the quiet and sanity.

The peace was short-lived. Sergei gave up the truck driving job to again focus full-time on his used car export business. He began meeting regularly with some local Russian immigrants to discuss cars, often staying out all night drinking with them. One night, I was awakened by a call at about 3:00 a.m.

"Mrs. Krasilnikov?"

"I'm Deb Miller, but I'm married to Sergei Krasilnikov."

The voice continued. "This is the Carmel Police Department. Your husband was arrested for driving while under the influence of alcohol. He's a Russki, right?"

"Yes, officer, he's Russian but has lived in America for nearly ten years."

"He said he was out with some comrades. We picked him up as he was weaving down the road. If you're willing, you can post bail and collect him at the jail any time. If it were me, I'd let him think about it and get him in the morning."

Sergei would never say "comrades," but I looked in the bed, and yes, he was missing. This wasn't a dream. I took the officer's advice and reset my alarm to allow time for a jail run on my way to work the next day. I wondered, *Where was the jail, anyway?* This was not a location that nice girls like me were familiar with. As I drifted back to sleep, I asked, *Why now?* Since Lina left, everything had been going smoothly. No shouting. No fists in my face. The grand vacation with Ally. I was beginning to think this marriage might make it after all. I could tame the beast. Ally could have a father who wasn't a dangerous, raving maniac.

But I'd spoken too soon. After being in Russia for a few months, Lina returned without advance notice within days of his release from jail. How many times did I need to stress the importance of communication? It was maddening! And we were already on thin ice from the jail call. Why was I still married to this guy? Oh, right, because I couldn't entrust Ally's care to a criminal capable of kidnapping. And I thought I could change this man.

Lina took me aside. She said things had gone great in Russia, and she and her mom had enjoyed getting to know each other. Sergei had somehow forced Lina's return against their wishes. She asked me to speak to him about going right back.

I took a deep breath and approached Sergei. "It's August. Why can't she enjoy a short visit, swim in our pool, play with her neighborhood friends, and return to Russia before school starts in the fall?" I suggested. That's what she told me she wanted to do. She missed her mom. Lina mentioned how calm it was in Russia without her dad's shouting. An equally important consideration for me was that my three kids and the au pair also deserved a peaceful home.

"Sergei, this could be a win for everyone," I said. I was sure he might put another fist in my face if I told him how different he acted around his daughter—alternating between spoiling and screaming at her. For me, Lina was easier to take care of without Sergei around. There was a single set of rules for all the kids; she responded well and seemed comfortable and happy. And *his* behavior was acceptable when Lina was with her mom; Sergei left my kids to me, and there were no arguments. Things were like they had been when he visited before he and Lina moved to America permanently. But being around Sergei and Lina in combination was becoming impossible.

"Shut up! Lina is *my* daughter, and she stays," he screamed. His eyes were wild and his nostrils flared. I wished we'd installed a panic button during the truce, while we had the chance, so I could sound the alarm if needed. Hadley wasn't upstairs to save me this time. I leaned down and whispered to

Ally to take her Teletubbies to her room, saying I'd join her in a few minutes.

"Lina only has me, nobody else," he said.

"She has a mom," I replied. "And you can't just single her out all the time with all your affection. Kids notice when there's preferential treatment. Even Ally can see it."

"Ally has *you*," he said.

But it was Linochka he treated like a baby, not Ally. It was Lina's hand he held wherever we went. Sergei presented only her with new clothes and gifts. He slept next to her when the family shared hotel rooms. The other kids noticed this behavior, which only served to isolate his daughter from the pack. They reckoned that if she received special treatment from her father, why did they have to continue to go out of their way to treat her as an equal? I could see their point, and as time passed, I stopped encouraging them to do otherwise. Ally integrated into the pack with Hadley and Tyler. They were a team. Ally didn't require and did not receive any special treatment from Sergei. She was growing up to be as independent as my first two children.

We stood in the kitchen, where Sergei had threatened my life just a few months earlier. I remembered how much easier our lives had been long ago when Sergei lived here without Lina during the two tennis exchanges. And it had been heaven the summer when he and Lina lived with his friend Rishat. Perhaps a permanent solution could be for Lina to spend part of her time with her mom *every* year. That way, my kids and me would only have to deal with him treating her like a princess part-time. Maybe that custodial arrangement would appeal to everyone, including her mom.

Forget the Fairy Tale and Find Your Happiness

I needed to do something. Since I couldn't divorce Sergei, what choice did I have? I'd stopped the Russian Hotel by calling him out in front of his friends. I'd made him start contributing financially, but that only lasted for a few months. I knew he was making enough money from his little car business to afford an apartment again. Since Sergei only seemed to understand ultimatums, it was time for another one.

"Sergei, why can't Lina split her time between here and Russia with her mom? That's what she tells me is her dearest wish," I asked again.

"She want me!" he shouted. "Nobody but me. And I want her."

"Then you can have nobody but her. That's how you act anyway. The rest of us don't exist to you when she's around. You've made that clear. So, you have two choices. Either she returns to Russia for the fall semester, after a few weeks of vacation here in Indiana, or you need to move out to an apartment again. You left me before when Ally was only a baby. You can do it again. You have enough money now. You've been shipping a lot of cars. You haven't contributed anything to this household since Lina left six months ago. Go. Be together. She's asking to split her time with her mom, and if you say no, then she's all yours."

He'd never apologized for threatening my life or for his lack of communication. It might have made a difference in our marriage if he had learned to apologize and calmly negotiate household rules. But communication with Sergei was a futile exercise. Initially, he chose door number two and moved to a nearby apartment. But two months later, he and Lina disappeared into thin air on Halloween night in 1999 without saying goodbye. I guess there was a door number three.

January 2000

It took hours for the rescue team to extract me through the windshield on that icy winter day. I was still wearing a crown of glass shards in my hair when I arrived at the ER. I managed a weak smile when the doctor explained how fortunate I was to survive the crash with only two broken bones in my back that might need surgery and a leg injury that would require crutches and physical therapy. Tears of joy rolled down my face when I reached the kids by phone from my hospital bed that night. We were going to be okay.

There had been no response from Sergei, who had surfaced in Virginia, eleven hours away, weeks after he left. Mom left messages telling him about my crash, but he didn't respond. Didn't he at least wonder how young Ally was doing? Despite the fog of pain meds, I tried to reach him by phone from the hospital and couldn't understand why he didn't pick up. I wanted to hear his voice to comfort me. If he were here, he'd take care of me. When he still didn't surface, I worried that something terrible had happened or that he'd returned to Russia. Then I got mad.

What kind of husband deserts his wife? He didn't communicate for months after he left. Even after his wife's near-death accident and subsequent hospitalization, he was nowhere to be found. What type of man fails to be concerned about his

Forget the Fairy Tale and Find Your Happiness

young child's welfare in this situation? The same type of man who had mistreated his previous wives. It reinforced why I kept Ally's passport locked in a safe—so he couldn't easily steal her away from her mother and take her outside the country as he'd done with Lina.

Sergei finally showed up in Indiana three weeks after my car accident to attend a required visit with his probation officer. Those monthly visits were the only time we saw him anymore, and he never stayed more than twenty-four hours. We learned he was staying with Russian friends in Virginia.

Narcotics helped to numb my physical pain after the accident's initial shock wore off, but they didn't take away my heartache. It took me a lifetime and a near-fatal car crash to begin realizing my prince would not save the day or even share it. I'd have to forget the fairy tale and forge my own path. It would be up to me to create the opportunities I wanted for my kids.

SECTION V

I Will Ride

The Beast rescued Belle from the wolves, and the sand would have buried Jasmine in the hourglass if Aladdin hadn't rescued her. These women had minds of their own but still relied on men to rescue them. It was a turning point for women when the protagonist saved Captain John Smith in Pocahontas. She kept the peace but lost her man when she opted to stay with her tribe.

Disney followed with Mulan, Tiana, and Merida, then Anna and Elsa, Moana, and Raya. Prince Charming no longer saved the day—or the princess—in these later movies. The Disney princess image continued evolving to the point where no prince was required. These heroines were strong and proud young women who figured out how to reach their dreams <u>and</u> care for their loved ones. But this evolution didn't happen overnight.

CHAPTER 16

Finding the Courage

Mulan was willing to sacrifice everything for the safety and love of her family. She wore a disguise and kept to herself to fly under the radar in a man's world. It was a lonely path for a woman, and there were tough decisions to make along the way. Mulan worked hard and quickly rose to the top because of her skills and leadership. This warrior princess bet on herself, bravely rising to every challenge.

"The good news about having a broken back is that I get to spend more time at home," I joked with the kids about my injuries and the six weeks of recovery time after the car crash. "No commute."

"Yeah, Cummins finally figured out how to squeeze two more work hours a day from you," Tyler said. He was right; the usual driving time now went toward additional work.

I was determined not to let things slide. Despite strict instructions to rest for six weeks, I worked nonstop from my bedpost. Cummins's new CEO wanted to launch his vision for the company, and as director of marketing and communications, the launch fell squarely on my shoulders. I'd fought hard over the past few years to elevate the importance of both internal and external communication in the organization. While a broken back and injured leg kept me from driving to the office, they wouldn't stop me from orchestrating this launch. I could barely walk but could do the job by phone and online. I'd show them!

Six weeks after the accident, I was cleared to drive—just in time for the big launch event. I shed my crutches and suited up in a metal back brace strategically covered by a turtleneck and an expandable wrap jacket. I wanted to witness the fruits of my labor, such as the "drum lady" musician who would lead the maracas team exercise for all attendees. And I couldn't miss Second City's performance. I'd helped co-write a skit with the Chicago comedy troupe, taking a risk by adding inside humor to humanize our senior leaders. Months of my creative efforts, along with innovative ideas from an outside consultant, culminated in the launch. The CEO wanted a different kind of meeting to signal the significant changes planned at the company.

Executives flew in from all over the world. No one from the corporate office had seen me since the crash, although they had heard my voice on endless calls as we organized the grand event. It was easy to forget I'd been physically sidelined. Afterward, when a few of them hugged me to celebrate the overwhelming success of the launch, they could feel my back brace. Only then did they look beyond my brave face and question if I was still in pain. I certainly was, but the pride I felt at overcoming a near-fatal experience and not skipping a beat at work diminished the stabbing pain in my slowly healing back.

The absolute joy was telling the kids all about it. Even two-year-old Ally was excited to hear about the success, especially when she found the leftover maraca I'd stuffed in my purse for her. She had helped me pick out the colorful plastic shakers from a party catalog a few weeks earlier.

"We'll need more of those," I told my kids. "The CEO loved the launch of his new vision. Now he wants all forty thousand global employees to complete the training—and get a maraca. My next problem is how to take this show on the road. Today was just the beginning."

I had never set my sights on a particular job on the corporate ladder. I started in finance, then fell in love with marketing and communication by following my interest in tennis and helping with the exchange. I had never sat down and mapped out a career plan. Instead, I had been receptive to opportunities, built a great team, and worked hard, which caused doors to open.

My efforts at Cummins led to internal promotions and outside recognition like industry awards and national speaking invitations. They also landed me on the radar of headhunters. I soon received requests to interview for exciting positions at companies across the country. As if I wasn't busy enough caring for three kids and working a demanding job leading a global team, researching these job opportunities would take precious hours. When the headhunters first came calling, I responded that I wasn't interested in moving. I'd offer them the names of business acquaintances they could approach instead—always trying to be helpful. After all, my family was firmly settled in Carmel with great schools and sports, and I had a fantastic job. I never thought I'd live outside of Indiana.

Forget the Fairy Tale and Find Your Happiness

Yet there was something that drew me to one particular headhunter call. The job description precisely matched my role at Cummins, which I dearly loved. The salary and bonus package was *three times* what I earned at Cummins. Braces and babysitters plus private preschools and high schools cost a lot, and my family could use the money. Even scarier, someone had to pay for college—the best universities came at a steep price. I needed to take charge of things for the family if I wanted my kids to have a better life. My boss at Cummins admitted that while I was contributing at a VP level, Cummins would never elevate my director position to a VP. They wanted to de-emphasize corporate support roles like mine. The headhunter call offered a chance to be appropriately paid for my work. But before I agreed to an interview in another state, I talked with Scott.

"A headhunter called a few weeks ago with a VP opportunity in Lancaster, Pennsylvania—near Philly."

"Amish country," he said, smiling. "Well, you deserve the VP part, not the fresh country air. Who's it with?"

"Armstrong, the flooring company." We both knew I would need his approval to take Hadley and Tyler with me if I moved.

"Did they make you an offer?" he asked.

"No, there's another round of conversations and then an on-site if I advance as a semi-finalist. The salary range is tons more than I make now. But I wanted to see how you would feel about us moving that far away before I invest precious vacation time to check it out."

"Money talks. Go for it!" he urged.

Scott had always believed in my professional abilities. He knew a big jump in salary would be good for our original family of four—and we would always be a family, even if we were separated by divorce. Scott and his second wife were both engineers working at the same plant. They lived about a quarter of a mile away from us. His wife didn't mesh well with Hadley and Tyler, so the prospect of us moving might ease his home life. Scott didn't like conflict.

I also told Hadley and Tyler before I proceeded with the interview process. We made decisions together as a family, unlike how I'd been raised. I remember how awful it felt when my parents told me we were moving when I was in junior high. I didn't want to blindside my kids.

"You're saying this is a possibility . . . that we could end up leaving Carmel right before my senior year?" Hadley asked.

"Dad and I talked and agreed you could stay here to finish school if you want to and live with him. Or I've looked online, and there's a great school out there that you might like, Lancaster Country Day School." The kids had been in the gifted programs at Carmel's public schools for elementary and middle school. For college prep, Hadley attended a private high school. She was doing great academically and was the star of her tennis team. If it came to pass, this move would create a dilemma for her.

"You're asking me to choose between you and Dad," she said.

My work laptop was on the kitchen table, open to the proposed school's home page.

Tyler immediately noticed. "They've got a hockey team! And tennis. Tons of AP classes, Hadley. You'd like it. And it starts at kindergarten, so Ally could go in a year, right after Hadley graduates."

Forget the Fairy Tale and Find Your Happiness

Ally heard her name and joined in the conversation. "I'm going with Mommy," she said firmly, looking to me for reassurance.

"Of course you are," I said, hugging Ally. "No one would ever ask you to choose between Dad and me, Hadley. I know the possibility of moving for your senior year is not good timing for you. I don't even know if I will be offered the job. I just wanted to give you time to start thinking it through. If the job becomes an option, we can always say no."

"How much did they offer you?" Tyler probed.

"There is no exact offer yet, just a range. But let's say it would be enough to make sending you guys to any college much easier. And to pay for braces," I said, looking at Tyler's teeth, knowing that was my next financial worry.

"I'm in!" he declared, shutting the laptop's lid, satisfied that this would be a good move for him. He was already mentally prepared to begin ninth grade in a new state.

Despite Tyler's enthusiasm, I knew this would be a tough transition if we chose to go forward. The Pennsylvania school seemed unique and excellent for college prep and athletics. We could consolidate the kids in one location rather than sending them to different schools all over town. In Indiana, it took me thirty minutes to drive Ally to preschool before driving another hour to work. And I held my breath as my teenager drove across town in the other direction on a busy highway to her high school. Next year, Tyler would join her. I was relieved when Hadley reluctantly agreed to do some research and pledged to keep an open mind until we knew whether I would receive an offer.

It saddened me to think of living even one year without Hadley in my home if she decided to stay in Indiana, but I also considered the challenge of future college expenses. My kids were bright and deserved the best education. They wanted it too. Hadley dreamed of grad school in the UK, and Tyler wanted to attend law school. I wanted to offer Ally similar opportunities, so I went to the effort of driving her across town to the gifted preschool that succeeded the Butler University program—the place that had sparked the dream of outstanding education for my kids. This job opportunity could be life-changing.

I decided my image was ready for an upgrade and stopped at Macy's the day before the interview in Pennsylvania. Sadly, my bland, dark wool suit wardrobe still reflected my working women's mentality from the '70s. Back then, we were supposed to blend in and follow along like good girls. *Don't look feminine, or they'll think you're incapable or a flirt.* I had accepted that expectation. But camouflaged or not, I knew I was more capable than most of the guys at work. I was interviewing for a vice president position. As a female, I'd stand out regardless of my appearance; I may as well *like* the outfit. I bought a chic collarless Calvin Klein suit in a stretchy champagne-colored fabric to wear for the interview. I felt like a million dollars. The bright mesh top I wore underneath had broad cranberry, orange, and fuchsia stripes that would make Mama Dell proud. As one of three finalists, I was ready for the competition in this new armor.

There were first-class tickets and limousines to get me to Armstrong headquarters. I could tell the first few interviewers were screening to decide if I would be a worthy candidate to introduce to their CEO while I was on-site. I must've passed their test because they added a final interview to the day so we could meet. The Armstrong CEO was a former top GE executive who had been considered to replace GE's Jack Welch.

His opening question was, "You have an eclectic background. How is it that a CPA becomes head of global marketing and communications at a Fortune 100 firm?"

"It started with tennis and led to Budweiser beer. Then I figured out how to creatively market diesel engines."

"Not a classic career path. So, you chose marketing over finance?" the CEO asked.

"It's a lot more fun."

"Chapter 11 can be fun too," he countered. "Are you aware of our asbestos issue?"

I nodded. I'd read the analyst reports. There was a significant legacy asbestos issue, and the reports implied that Chapter 11 was the only way to resolve the company's mounting claims. From my CPA experience and my previous role leading investor relations at Cummins, I knew that Chapter 11 meant a complete reorganization. The new owners typically replaced top leadership.

"A reorganization is planned . . . and soon. And yes, most of the leadership positions, including this new one, will be eliminated at some point down the road," he shared. He went on, "Any offer of employment would address this challenge, and officers of the company will be well compensated for the uncertainty of their employment."

That explained the position's salary range: high risk, high reward.

"Does that scare you?" he asked.

"If you're good, you can always find another job," I responded. I liked his transparency.

"And you're good." He stated my implication.

"Cummins thinks so."

"I suppose so. They promoted you pretty quickly," he said, reviewing my résumé.

The interview went well. We saw eye to eye; as a new CEO, he had a new vision to communicate, just like I'd recently done at Cummins.

My return flight touched down at the airport in Indiana after midnight in the midst of a blizzard. My car was buried in snow like a frozen pumpkin. I dug out and carefully drove home to sleep for a couple of hours. By 6:00 a.m., it was back to work—"on press" at the printer with Cummins's annual report. It felt like the interview trip had never happened . . . until I got the call.

"Hey, Deb." It was Armstrong's HR VP. "You're going to receive an offer package tomorrow by courier, but let me tell you—we want you on the Armstrong team."

It didn't feel real until that package arrived. I ripped open the cardboard envelope and was instantly overcome when I read the numbers on the page. I felt lightheaded, as if all the air had been released. I staggered from the kitchen to the big chair in the great room to take a seat. It was one thing to hear over the phone that an offer was coming. It was quite another to read that my future and my children's futures could be financially secure. This was my dream! A lifetime of studying and hard work was finally paying off. I would have a seat at the table as one of the top ten executives of a Fortune 500 organization.

I'd finally made it. It was an overwhelming rush of feelings. Accomplishment. Validation. Pride. And complete and utter joy.

Mom fully supported my move—her daughter would be a vice president! I still had to measure the cost of uprooting my family, especially Hadley. In Hadley's mind, any decision sent a message to the parent she didn't choose to live with, making it impossible for her to decide. So, she left it to Scott and me. Armstrong's generous offer gave us multiple housing visits to make such decisions. Hadley and Tyler spent a day shadowing at the prospective school. I visited several preschools as Ally would need one for at least one more year. There were some palatable options, all without the long drive we had back in Indy. Ally's true gift was her outgoing personality. She would bloom anywhere.

And there was still that Chapter 11 catch. The fact that the company was about to be reorganized meant my position would be eliminated at some point when the company emerged from that process. Did I want to take a job knowing I'd be gone in a few years? This was a significant risk. Could I find another VP job and then put the family through another move when that happened?

The final consideration was that moving to the East Coast would put us a mere three hours from Sergei. He'd left Ally and me more than a year ago. Following the months of silence, including those first few weeks after my crash, he'd begun to call regularly. Then he started having monthly visits with his Indiana probation officer—the result of his DUI arrest. He'd act as if nothing had happened on each trip, ignoring that he lived eleven hours away. He'd stay for one night and expected full marital relations. What if we lived closer to him?

Armstrong's recruiting team wanted an answer. They were trying hard to close the deal with me. They'd arranged the school visit for the kids and wanted me to look at local housing on a second trip. They assumed my husband needed a flight too. I wasn't sure what to do. We weren't divorced, yet I didn't want Sergei to perceive this move as an attempt at reconciliation.

On the other hand, my ever-optimistic side wondered if our separation had changed him. Either way, I couldn't hide the news if I moved from Indiana. I had to call him.

"Sergei, I will be in Pennsylvania tomorrow for two days. There's a job I'm looking at, and the company wants me to meet with a real estate agent to check out some houses."

"I will meet you there, Deb. I am so happy!"

I hadn't even asked, but it was typical of him to dive in headfirst. "I'll be there tomorrow for two days," I repeated, wishing the job offer was on the West Coast. I would not just let him walk back into our lives. I knew I had to be strong. But two facts remained: I couldn't divorce him due to custody concerns, and, if I was honest with myself, a part of me still loved the man who took my breath away when he entered the room.

Sergei greeted me at the hotel in Lancaster, smiling broadly and holding flowers. He could hardly contain his excitement. When we got to the door of our room, he picked me up and kicked in the door, announcing, "This is honeymoon!"

"Sergei, we need to talk. If I take . . ."

"No talking! You talk too much," he said, ready to start the honeymoon.

Forget the Fairy Tale and Find Your Happiness

It was the first time the two of us had been alone together at a hotel since we married—no family of five or six sharing a room like usual. Sergei was in his forties and had aged well. We both had. We shared a beautiful child. During our separation, I tried hard to see things from his viewpoint. I could never forgive him for leaving us, but I did sympathize with his situation as a single parent.

"If we do move to Pennsylvania, it doesn't mean we can live together again with you and Lina. That didn't work for any of us." I held firm. The kids would be proud.

"Okay. Anything," Sergei agreed. "But only if you stop talking right now."

Sergei was silent the next day while the real estate agent drove us around town. He understood he didn't have a vote on housing. I recognized that everything we said would be relayed back to Armstrong. We stuck to the facts. Sergei lived in Virginia. He coached at JTCC, a top tennis academy in the DC area. It was understood that he wouldn't leave a top coaching job to join us in a small town in Pennsylvania if I accepted.

Ultimately, my decision to accept the offer was based on what was best for my kids. A little more than a year after the car accident, I started the new job as a vice president, not knowing that moving closer to Sergei was also moving me closer to the truth.

Despite the excitement of the move, there were also challenges. It was difficult to leave the only home the kids had ever known. I decided to rebuild a house for us in Pennsylvania that was nearly identical to our home in Indiana. Childcare was also a struggle. Finding someone you can trust in a new community is incredibly challenging. I flew my mom out to Pennsylvania to help for the first few days. Over the weekend, we drove with Ally to Toronto, where we collected Melissa, who had been our third au pair. She'd arrived from Australia around the time Sergei abandoned us and was with us during my recovery from the car crash. We'd become good friends during those challenging times, and all three kids loved her. We considered Melissa a permanent part of our family. We'd always stay in touch. She was flying back for a month to help us settle in Pennsylvania.

Melissa's visa was initially rejected due to bureaucratic nonsense, so we figured out a work-around. As an Australian, she could quickly fly to Canada. We'd pick her up there and drive back to Pennsylvania. Unfortunately, we were stopped at the Canada–US border. Melissa and I were whisked inside to offices we'd never imagined entering. Now, I imagined our mug shots.

They separated Melissa and me to ask questions. We didn't think we'd done anything wrong. We hadn't prepared any excuse and told the truth of the matter. Melissa was trying to help me acclimate Ally to our new state as a favor. She loved Ally. We weren't trying to displace an American worker, and we weren't human trafficking. It was an unpaid visit. It wasn't long before my mom burst into the border patrol office building with Ally, who promptly began turning cartwheels in the lobby. Mom had exhausted her ability to entertain a preschooler in the car. I think the US immigration team felt sorry for me. Ally sold the deal by trying to kiss Melissa through the glass pane of her interrogation room. They approved Melissa's entry, and we were back on our way. With the fear of detention behind us, we stopped at nearby Niagara Falls to celebrate.

Forget the Fairy Tale and Find Your Happiness

I approached our East Coast experience as if we were exchange students—only as a family unit. I knew my job was short-lived due to Armstrong's Chapter 11, and we had limited time to see this part of the country. We took advantage of exploring the region with weekend trips to Washington, DC, Gettysburg, Cape May, Philadelphia, and even Atlantic City. Hadley visited prospective colleges in New England. We took the train to New York City and hung out at the US Open.

Sergei racked up his own mileage with random visits to Pennsylvania every few weeks. He was thrilled that we now lived much closer, an unintended consequence of our move, and was typically on good behavior. I tried to make his brief visits a happy time for Ally. To her, it was normal that her dad was absent most of the time.

"How's my baby?" he'd exclaim, scooping her up and smothering her with kisses, ignoring the fact that he'd deserted his youngest daughter.

"How's my mommy?" He'd wrap his strong arms around me and try to will the three of us to be as one—at least for a few hours. His visits were always a surprise. I had to adjust my mind each time, trying not to criticize another lack of communication but needing to calculate how to include him in our plans.

"Sergei, why do you always arrive at dawn and return by midnight?"

"That's the only way the old people will babysit," he said. Years ago, he'd ruined his credit when he broke his lease in Indiana. He couldn't rent an apartment in Virginia, so he said he'd found an elderly Russian couple who rented out the lower level of their townhouse to Sergei and Lina. These people babysat

Lina when he visited us in Pennsylvania, but he said they had limitations.

"They used to watch her overnight when you drove to Indiana. This rule didn't apply back then. And isn't Lina asleep at midnight anyway?" I asked. "She's thirteen years old."

"We can move to Pennsylvania and live with you," he responded. He knew I wasn't agreeable to that. Our home was happy without having him around full-time. The kids and I all remembered how awful it had been living with the two of them, and we wanted no part of it. I couldn't take that risk for my kids' safety and happiness or my sanity.

In addition to the odd hours of his occasional visits, he began using phrases I'd never heard from him before. When I turned him down for a quick rendezvous before he hit the road, he said, "Our relationship is going nowhere." Soon after, this man with broken English who had never expressed interest in marital communications suggested we try "relationship counseling." I sensed someone or something was driving his change in vocabulary. I hired a detective to learn more. But after only receiving confirmation of where he lived and where he coached tennis, accompanied by a $1,500 bill, I gave up on professional help. I decided to look him up on my own the next time I was on business in Washington, DC. I drove the rental car to his landlord's Virginia townhouse, where Sergei rented the lower level. I sat in the car as light snow fell, staring at the front door, waiting for someone to emerge. The lights were on. I looked around. So this is where he placed calls; he always seemed to be walking the landlord's dog outside when we spoke. That night I was too cold to stay longer, and I was too chicken to knock on the door. I left after an hour.

My next move was to access his email account. After all, he'd asked me to set it up years ago and had never changed the password. Nothing there. Sergei was still on my monthly phone bill, so I checked his call log. There were many calls to his landlord and other known Russian contacts. That's it. I didn't like myself for doing these things. But the lack of trust was eating me alive. I sensed he was leading a double life. Without trust, how could I truly love him?

My suspicions motivated me to hire an attorney in Pennsylvania to see if different custody rules might apply. No, but she helped me draft a formal will that stipulated my wishes for Ally's care in the event of my death. Hadley, nearly eighteen now, was named guardian out of concern for Sergei's temper and abandonment. I feared that nomination would never hold up in court and lost sleep many nights, worrying about what would happen to Ally if I wasn't there to take care of her. Sergei was not reliable. The lawyer also advised me to list the kids as my beneficiaries on my growing list of investments. For the first time, I had money left after paying the monthly bills. It felt great, and I was investing it for my kids' future. As my spouse, Sergei had to sign off on these beneficiary designations. This was easy. He always signed things without reading them.

We were happy in Pennsylvania. Hadley won the state doubles tennis title, the first state championship for her school. She was selected to participate in Model United Nations and spent a week at The Hague with her new friends. She had her first boyfriend and looked like a princess when they went to the prom. Tyler excelled in the smaller classrooms with demanding teachers. He could participate in sports—hockey and soccer, and he even joined the golf team. He learned to drive. Tapping into Sergei's auto auction connections, we added a used Land Rover and a used Miata convertible to our household fleet—dream vehicles for my teenagers.

Ally busied herself by making friends everywhere she went, collecting marriage proposals and pets along the way. She excelled with the local swim team, and Hadley began giving her tennis lessons. Ally assigned a Care Bear name to each of us. Hadley was "Sister Bear," Tyler was "Grizzly Bear," and I was "Worker Bear." It was depressing to hear, but I accepted my role as the family's provider. Soon, Hadley would be off to college, and we'd be breaking up the Care Bear family. Letting go of her would be one of the most challenging things I'd ever do.

Lesson 16—Be Brave

Amherst College's orientation for students and parents had concluded, and it was time to leave Hadley behind. The multi-day sessions had effectively spread the pain of separation and probably reduced the intensity of our emotions. There had been no emotion when my parents left me at college decades earlier, but these few days of transition helped Hadley and me work through the pain of our impending separation. With each orientation session, I gained more strength to face the inevitable—our core family would never be the same again. I took one last look at her dorm room, now fully decorated with help from Pottery Barn, like a small slice of home.

The three days at Amherst flew by. Hadley and I agreed not to say goodbye curbside. It would be too emotional for us. She waved from a distance. When I lifted Ally into her car booster seat, she saw my tears.

Forget the Fairy Tale and Find Your Happiness

"Don't be sad, Mommy," said my youngest, the optimist. "I was worried about starting kindergarten next week, but Hadley said you taught her to be brave, and you'd teach me too."

I was glad to have Ally there to help me get through this. She'd be at home for another twelve years. Without her, I'm not sure I would've had the strength to pull away from that curb.

Ally added, "Hadley said she wants to be just like you, Mommy. Me too."

An ultimate test of bravery came two years after our move to Pennsylvania when Armstrong eliminated my job, along with most of the other VP positions, as the company began emerging from Chapter 11. Even though I'd expected it, it was still a shock. I'd never lost a job. There was no time to feel sorry for myself; I had to provide for my family. A mortgage. A car payment. Soon, *two* kids in college. My kingdom was threatened, but I still had an outstanding reputation. I'd reached the level of VP, and there was no way I would settle for anything less. It took courage and about eight months, but I found another executive position, this time with The Timken Company.

Tyler and Ally seemed thrilled with our move to Ohio. Tyler became a member of the academic bowl and ice hockey teams at his new school, an unusual combination. Ally quickly became the queen of her class, just as she'd done in Pennsylvania, winning students' and teachers' hearts with her sunny personality. At home, she spent hours jumping on the trampoline in our backyard—ever the daredevil. We joined a country club that offered golf and a swimming team in the summer and tennis year-round. The kids continued their idyllic childhood.

It was a surprising transition for me. On the surface, the position at Timken looked like the Cummins job I had loved, only with the chance to be an SVP and earn a six-figure pension. And I worked for another new CEO with a new vision, my third in a row. I was an expert. Additionally, both Cummins and Timken were in the automotive and industrial component business—one primarily engines and the other bearings—as "ingredient" engineering and manufacturing organizations with global operations. Underneath it all, however, the companies' cultures could not have been more different. J.I. Miller from Cummins had famously helped organize Martin Luther King Jr.'s March on Washington for civil rights. At Timken, leaders like me were strong-armed to support selected candidates of a certain political party. I would vote for whomever I wanted to behind the closed curtain, but it was time to start thinking about my next move if I wanted to reach my professional happily ever after. Like Dad had told me long ago, if you're good, you can always find another job.

CHAPTER 17

Finding the Truth

Subjected to the witch's lies, a naive Rapunzel was trapped in a tower for years. She dreamed of a happier future and tried to make the best of a bad situation. Eventually, the power of the truth set her free, with an assist from her long, beautiful tresses.

Sergei's periodic visits continued when the kids and I moved to Ohio. When he was in town, he began playing tennis with Ally and marveled at her natural ability. He hadn't been interested when she was younger, but now that her strokes were taking shape, her tennis game caught his attention. Ally had started in Barbara's Tot Tennis in Indiana, where preschoolers have fun and learn to love the game. Then Hadley worked with her in Pennsylvania and taught her the fundamentals. Ally began group instruction at local clubs when her sister went to college. She was competitive and loved to play with other kids. Sergei complained about the quality of the group coaching, but I think he was just jealous because he was missing out.

On one of his visits to Ohio, he left his email account open on my desktop computer after he left for Virginia. The headline at the top of his page caught my attention.

Subject: CNN.com—Study finds frequent sex cuts cancer risk—Apr. 7

Upon closer look, I saw that a woman had sent the email. What? This was a red flag I could not ignore. More like a flashing red light! I boldly emailed the sender from my email account and asked why she would send my husband an article about frequent sex. Like Betsy before her, this woman responded to me. Natasha was Russian, half of the "old couple" with the townhouse who had rented space to Sergei for years. His landlord! Natasha's ex-husband had moved out just as Sergei and Lina moved into the lower floor of the townhome. I also learned she wasn't as old as he'd described. Natasha was approximately the same age as Sergei and me. She knew we were married, but they'd been having an affair for over four years! He was a tenant with benefits.

"He told me *you* were an old woman," she shared. And so began another cycle of disbelief, pain, and follow-up with the other woman to learn the shocking details. I knew he wouldn't tell me the truth but thought Natasha might—as Betsy had. She did. She even offered this advice: "You just need to give him a lot of sex and don't let him stay out of your sight."

After a few painful email exchanges, I recognized some of the verbiage and realized Natasha had been giving Sergei advice about *their* relationship, which he later tried out with *me*. She said she'd begged him to go to "relationship counseling" because their relationship was "going nowhere." That advice wasn't the only thing he'd passed on to me from Natasha. A few years back, I'd developed a horrible case of what the gynecologist diagnosed as genital herpes. I had only slept with two men in my life, my husbands. How had I developed herpes? Only now did that diagnosis make sense. Sergei had led a double life!

I wanted to blame the detective I'd hired when we lived in Pennsylvania for not discovering this situation hiding in plain sight. But I'd missed it too. I might have been able to figure out they were having an affair if I'd knocked on their door that snowy night and discovered there was no "old couple" as landlords. Maybe I'd been afraid of what I might find out—the truth.

Natasha explained her midnight restriction on Sergei's visits to Pennsylvania. The intended purpose was to ensure that he wasn't in my bed. She thought Sergei's timely return to Virginia fulfilled his promise to Natasha that he'd only visit his young daughter, Ally, and not have a relationship with me. I guess she was stupid too. Natasha should've realized a curfew wouldn't stop Sergei from trying to initiate sex with his wife. He'd remained aggressive since our first kiss long ago.

Learning all this was paralyzing. They say the truth will set you free. But it froze me. Sergei had lived with someone else for more than four years! He'd even been on family vacations with both families over the years. I didn't talk to anyone about this atrocity because it was too embarrassing. It hurt. Badly. And I couldn't divorce this asshole because of the custody issue! Ally was too young.

I reflected on the advice I'd received from Russian women over the years. I'd consulted with a few acquaintances about Sergei's infidelity to understand if it was cultural or just him.

One woman advised, "It's the lady's job to keep the man happy."

Another said, "Only once did I see a successful marriage when the woman earned the larger income. A Russian man's ego can't handle that." That was our biggest challenge, she thought.

When I initially confronted him about his adultery, he retorted, "Do you have a problem? I don't have a problem."

He implied that he had permission to cheat because we no longer blended our families under one roof. But when I was pregnant with Ally and he had lived with us (along with his two daughters), it didn't stop him from trying to cheat with Betsy. Whenever we'd dared to discuss the possibility of recombining our families, Sergei had vetoed any guidelines. He wanted his family members and friends to be able to live with us full-time and come and go without any communication—the Russian Hotel. And he would not agree to contribute to the family financially. I did not accept those conditions. And he wouldn't take any blame for his transgressions, either then or now. No apology. Quite the opposite.

"This is *your* fault," he stated matter-of-factly to justify his actions.

A few days after I discovered Natasha's email, Sergei changed his tune. He declared his love; he wanted me to untie my tubes and have another baby with him. My response was to have the security company change the locks on our Ohio home. Good thing, because Natasha emailed me to say he'd extended her the same offer of fatherhood. I could have written this entire script. It was the rerun of a *Betsy* episode from season one. So, I repeated my lines from that script the next time he called.

"Sergei, it's over."

"Deb, I know you have many men while I'm in Virginia. You are a beautiful woman. You don't sit alone. You take many men to bed," Sergei said.

I was shocked! Was he crazy? That hurt. I guess he was unable to imagine that someone *wouldn't* cheat if they had the opportunity. "Sergei, you know I would never, ever do that."

"Then you must be a lesbian!" he said. Sergei questioned how any woman could refuse to have sex with him as frequently as he desired and could go without it in his absence. This man was out of control. He switched tactics again. "I'm driving to Ohio right now."

"You'll have to stay at a hotel after you drive the six hours to get here," I informed him. "I changed the locks. You're no longer welcome here."

I knew he'd never spring for a hotel, and he didn't show up. His next move was to go silent for a while, hoping I would cool off and soften my position. After all, that strategy had worked for him in the past. Meanwhile, he kept busy trying to reconcile with Natasha. She was reportedly not interested. "He can't carry on an intelligent conversation about anything besides tennis or used cars," she claimed.

I had to carry on. The kids kept me going, and work kept me sane. I worked even harder. For some, this kind of personal revelation would have impacted the quality of their work or their relationships with their kids. For me, it did not. I always compartmentalized the situation and put the pain on a shelf—until the next time or until Ally reached eighteen years old.

Yet I wondered who else knew. I felt like a fool. Why hadn't anyone told me he was doing these things? I guess Betsy had long ago, that day of the sonogram. Did it matter? I'd stayed with him. I wondered if he ever loved me. I'd never asked if Scott loved me. I just knew. And he knew I loved him—even after we were no longer *in* love. I wondered, had I ever loved Sergei? Or had I simply wanted him? Because I was raised to think I needed to marry anyone I had sex with, I felt bound to marry Sergei. I'd let society's expectations guide my life decisions.

Sergei no longer held my heart, but he had power over me as long as Ally was a minor. I couldn't divorce him because of society's rules about custody. What would I do for the next ten years? I started having recurring nightmares where Ally was abused while she visited Sergei and some girlfriend he kept in another state. And in one dream, the couple moved to Russia and took Ally from me. No, I could never leave my child with him.

It wasn't just her safety that concerned me; I didn't want to have a second divorce on my record either. Society would frown upon me for that. I remembered how it was when Scott and I divorced. Our friends were all couples. A single divorced woman was excluded.

Sergei called and spoke with Ally when I was at work. He asked how her tennis lessons were going. She played in local tournaments, and he was dying to hear about her progress. Sergei left voicemails, professing his undying love for Ally and me. Sergei's sister had a successful business in Russia and had given him money to buy a condo in Virginia. He lived there now. Lina was occupied with her boyfriend. Sergei was lonely and pleaded with me to let him back into our lives. I could never forgive Sergei for his long affair, but after about a year of separation, I agreed to stay married. I didn't see any other option. "Every child needs a father," Mom taught me. I would tough this out for Ally. Ten years to go.

There was a condition to our reconciliation: Sergei had to move to Ohio to live with Ally and me. (Tyler was now in college.) Lina was eighteen, and her boyfriend stayed with her in the Virginia condo. I'd try to make it work, but that effort would come with a new personal condition. I had to be tipsy, if not drunk, to share his bed. The main reason for the alcohol was that I didn't like myself—I was that woman who stayed married to a cheater. I didn't respect her. Sex also became painful as I entered menopause.

Sergei had a condition too. He wanted to coach Ally in tennis, but only if I paid him a full salary to coach her two hours a day. Our child united us, and we also shared a dream that Ally could become an outstanding tennis player.

Now that Sergei and I lived together, we slowly rebuilt our lives as a unit of three. Sergei continued his used car business and pocketed the profits, along with his coaching payments from me, enjoying a life without expenses. Meanwhile, much of my income went to providing Tyler with a nice education at Northwestern University and Ally with a nice home. With just the three of us, there were few arguments. It was nice to have a co-parent to take some pressure off me. Sergei even accompanied me to a conference in Singapore. We took Ally to France, where I had meetings, and to Russia, where I delivered a presentation in Russian—with a translation assist from Sergei. While there, we took a side trip to Chelyabinsk and attended his high school reunion as a family. In Moscow, we attended the Kremlin Cup pro tennis event. Sergei obtained credentials and Ally hung out with the players. We sat right behind Maria Sharapova in business class on the flight home. She and Ally joined forces to entertain a one-year-old passenger who snuggled in the lap of her new adoptive mother during the flight.

Ally and Sergei worked on her tennis game daily wherever we traveled. When we visited Moscow, she jumped into top tennis clinics and worked with legendary Russian coaches thanks to Sergei's connections. While these were work trips for me, the side events provided an escape from the pressure of my job. Once, I left my briefcase home and we enjoyed a Caribbean cruise with Ally, punctuated with pretty tropical drinks. It was a glorious time.

Sergei seemed to enjoy the country club life. And Ally was always happy, especially when we got a dog, Muffin. I thought Sergei had changed, and maybe we'd make it as a couple. Our shared dream for Ally's success in tennis became a reality. She did well at the Little Mo tournament in Arizona for the nation's top seven- and eight-year-olds. But Sergei wasn't satisfied with Ally's competition options in Ohio. He insisted that she needed to hit with other top kids. He lobbied for us to move to Florida. I couldn't leave my job, so we invited top older kids from Cleveland to train with her on the weekends. They came to work with Sergei, and Ally was the beneficiary. We also brought over a twenty-year-old sparring partner from Russia because Sergei wanted someone else to hit with Ally so he could stand next to her and coach. He insisted she needed to train regularly in Florida with other top national prospects of similar age, like Ally's dear tennis friend Sonya Kenin, whom we'd met during a Florida vacation when Ally was seven.

Forget the Fairy Tale and Find Your Happiness

It was never smooth sailing with Sergei for very long. The more Ally improved, the more argumentative he became on the court and at home.

"She not listen to me!" he reported.

"He's psycho!" Ally told me. "I don't know what he wants. He doesn't explain anything and then yells at me when I don't do it his way. He screams on the court, hits balls at me, and then takes me for ice cream and acts all lovey afterward. He's not normal!"

"She don't want to play tennis," Sergei said.

"I don't want to play with *him*!" Ally replied.

It was tough to listen to them. Sergei, with his stern Soviet approach, didn't understand how to effectively coach an American girl. Sergei's coaching in Ohio was helping our daughter develop good technique and reach the top echelon of junior tennis for her age group, but at what price? I knew she'd quit if they kept training together in Ohio, and they'd hate each other.

"I just received a big bonus," I told Sergei one day. "What would you think if we made a down payment on a vacation home in Florida, a base for Ally's training? She could be with other kids and coaches."

"I could train at Saviano's academy! Or with Sonya!" Ally said. "Away from Dad!"

"Florida! A place like Barbara's." Sergei smiled.

"Well, we can't afford a big place on the beach like Barbara and John used to have. Maybe a small condo. But Ally, you could train outdoors year-round like Dad keeps insisting is important," I said. I wanted Ally to feel at home and not always live out of a suitcase.

I made the investment. We had a tenant to help defer the cost of the mortgage. I thought Hadley and Tyler could enjoy the house too. At first, we used the vacation home sporadically, tied to training for the big national tournaments in Florida and during school holidays. There were many top coaches in South Florida with academies that welcomed Ally. She usually received free training, especially if Sergei helped out with other players. Ally was relieved she didn't have to spend as much time training with Sergei as she'd done in Ohio. She worked hard and became a top national prospect based on tournament results, ranking as high as number two in the country. Babolat sponsored Ally. Then Nike. Boxes with racquets, clothes, and shoes began to arrive quarterly, each time filling an entire room.

It wasn't long before the USTA invited Ally to train part-time at its prestigious national training center in Boca Raton, Florida, less than a mile from our vacation home. The catch was that she'd have to live locally and attend school in Florida. Ally was sad to leave her school friends in Ohio but excited to join her tennis friends in Florida. Sergei was ecstatic. I didn't think we could pass up this opportunity for her future. I kept my job, which funded this dream, and commuted every weekend from Ohio. Their move meant Sergei lived with Ally unchaperoned during the week.

Now that Sergei and I faced another physical separation, old patterns reemerged. First, the return of the Russian Hotel, Florida edition. Sometimes this was good, like when Sergei's Russian tennis friends, also coaches, brought their kids to train, including Sascha Zverev, Roman Safiullin, and Christina

Makarova. But mostly, his Russian business buddies and family members came for monthlong vacations in the sun, with free room and board on Deb's tab.

Sergei's attraction to other women also resurfaced after he moved to Florida. While the cat is away, the mouse will play. As usual, it took me a while to catch on. Ally alerted me to a female tennis coach who frequently came over to drink bottles of gin and sometimes crashed for the night. And Ally reported being left at a hotel pool with a young Russian girl while Sergei and the girl's mother disappeared for a few hours.

He, of course, acted like nothing had happened. "You're crazy, Deb."

Fundamentally, Sergei and I had different values. I'd never forgiven him for Betsy or Natasha. I couldn't give myself freely to him because I didn't trust him in our relationship. I no longer worried Sergei would steal Ally away to Russia as she could speak for herself. But I still feared joint custody. That was always the showstopper. And we shared the dream of her success in tennis. I didn't want to ruin her future because I couldn't get along with Sergei. The optimist in me still believed I could fix him.

I knew my weekday absence in Florida wasn't ideal, but I was in the final months of earning a future pension and couldn't relocate without that sacrifice. My family needed the lifelong financial independence my pension would provide. I knew Sergei was a bum, but I didn't think his behavior would harm Ally, only me. I pleaded with him to set a better example for our daughter and keep her safe while I was working up north. He didn't have to coach every day, and Ally benefited from training with other top kids in Florida, which is what he said he wanted. I was treading water, working hard all week, and commuting eight hours each way on weekends. There were no direct flights. I could leave my job and rejoin my child full-time in a few months.

One day, Ally called me sobbing—the first time I'd heard her cry. Sergei had become angry about her lack of performance on the court earlier that day. He'd hit tennis balls at her and struck her so hard with a hat it left welts. Then he drove away, leaving her at the neighborhood courts.

"Sergei! You hit our child! And purposely locked her out of the house in that hot sun! She sat alone for hours on the front porch. Hurt, hungry, and thirsty. Scared to death!"

"She not listen to me. She don't want to play tennis," was his only explanation. No apology for his unacceptable behavior. It was always someone else's fault.

It wouldn't be easy to leave work then; we were announcing quarterly results, and I had no backup. I arranged for Ally to stay at a friend's home for two days and called my mom. At eighty-three years old, she didn't hesitate. She grabbed a buddy and they drove a thousand miles to stay for a few weeks—which Mom viewed as a lovely extended spring break in sunny Florida. I didn't tell Mom what Sergei had done. Mom instinctively took over, and I continued to come to Florida on the weekends until Ally's school concluded the spring semester. Ally, Mom, and I ignored Sergei and enjoyed the time together. I brought Ally back to Ohio with me for the summer. Sergei tagged along, insisting on overseeing her training. Ally and I agreed, but *only* if there could be a third person on the court with them at all times or if he just took her to tournaments. With my pension now secured, I began the process of leaving my job and moving to Florida with Ally for her continued tennis training with the USTA. I thought her future might be in tennis, and I wanted Ally to have that opportunity. I also started looking for a Florida family law attorney—to be ready for next time.

In the fall of 2010, Ally turned thirteen. She was good enough to be one of only three American girls her age invited to train full-time at the USTA's national center. She wanted to train there with her friends—and to entirely escape Sergei's involvement in her tennis. To participate in the program, Ally had to commit to online schooling through the USTA's partner, Kaplan. I was concerned about her education as Hadley and Tyler always attended top schools. Ally had too—up until this point. But accepting the USTA's offer meant Sergei would be entirely out of her coaching picture. I sold our home in Ohio, where Ally and Tyler had been so happy. I began living and working in Florida, where I could monitor her education and training and, most importantly, keep Ally safe.

Ally grew six inches that year. Like a retriever puppy, you could tell she would continue to grow. The USTA asked her young body to play from morning until evening six to seven days a week and do the same conditioning as a professional woman. After months of overtraining and forty-five straight days of playing under the direction of an inexperienced coach at USTA's national training center, the muscles in Ally's young neck locked up and she was in extreme pain. She attempted to serve mid-match against Jenny Brady, a top player who was full-grown and years older than Ally. But her neck froze and Ally couldn't raise her arm or move her head, or even her eyeballs. A highly trained athletic trainer who had previously worked on the ATP tour, Bill Norris, worked with her for years afterward for rehab. Bill compared the injury to whiplash in a bad car crash. Bill warned that Ally might never fully recover, especially mentally.

Sergei and I complained about the overtraining, and the USTA responded by demoting Ally from full-time training to only occasional coaching, a setback to her confidence and career. When Ally finally healed physically and felt like playing again, we found other places for her to train, although at a much-reduced schedule and with lesser results. She shifted to playing international tournaments, mostly away from the US junior tennis scene.

I found a job as vice president of marketing and communications at a large company in Miami, which meant another daily commute of more than a hundred miles, just as I'd had back in Indiana. At least there were no icy roads this time. Ally and I picked out a beautiful new neighborhood in Florida and built a permanent home to move into, much larger than our vacation home. We'd left our dog, Muffin, with our neighbors in Ohio, who took much better care of her than we could due to my previous commuting schedule. Now that we were fully settled in Florida, it was hard to say no when Ally rescued a miniature Chihuahua from Costa Rica, where she'd played a tennis tournament. Beanie soon stole our hearts.

Sergei was not as interested in Ally's tennis career after she left the USTA full-time program. He thought college tennis was for failures. Sergei had a "go pro or don't play" attitude. His dream for her to become a tennis pro died, and he blamed everyone but himself.

As he'd done in Virginia, he talked his wealthy sister into buying a condo in Florida as a rental investment. She visited only once. Sergei managed the property, but he rarely rented it out. It mainly served as his personal Russian hotel for a constant carousel of visiting friends in addition to the steady stream of guests he invited to stay at our home. Sergei enjoyed playing host.

I kept busy working in Miami and overseeing Ally's education—she continued to attend school online so she could travel for tennis. There were still trips to plan for her international tournaments, and I wanted to enjoy every minute with my youngest child while she was still home. Even after the injury, she was talented enough to earn a scholarship to play Division 1 tennis in college. Ally finished high school a year early, in the spring of 2015, and looked forward to joining the college scene that fall. It was tough when any of my kids went away to school, but losing my youngest would mark the end of the best and most important era of my life.

"I'm not leaving you alone, Mom. You have Beanie now. And you can come and watch my matches. You love that," Ally said. We were at T.G.I. Fridays in Boca Raton having dinner after I got home from work. "Hadley said she's flying out to help us to move me into the dorm this fall."

"Do you remember when we moved *her* in? You were not quite five."

"Yes," Ally said. "You cried. And you *never* cry."

"I was already dreading the day *you* would go to college. I may cry again."

"That's why Hadley is coming."

"I don't want to think about it tonight. What if we go by and help Dad clean out the condo?" Sergei had reportedly been working hard to clean his sister's unit before listing it for sale; he'd convinced her to upgrade and invest in a house in Florida, and the deadline was near. Sergei had even slept there the night before after cleaning all day. The condo was only half a mile from the restaurant. Ally agreed that we should go and help him out. When we pulled into the driveway, we noticed a Mercedes SUV alongside his car. That wasn't unusual; Sergei didn't like being alone and always invited his Russian buddies over. But the front door was locked, and that *was* odd; he rarely locked any door unless he was leaving overnight. We walked around back, where the sliding glass door was unlocked, and we stepped in.

Ally sprinted ahead. "Mom, whose shoes are these?" she asked, pointing to a pair of women's sandals beside Sergei's athletic shoes by the front door.

I didn't know whose shoes they were, but I knew what they meant. I could tell by the disgusted look on Ally's face that she knew too. I could no longer ignore Sergei's philandering—it was finally out in the open.

"Mom, it looks like they left in a hurry," she said from the kitchen, pointing to a pan of food still cooking on a lit burner. She boldly dashed toward the master bedroom near the rear door on the first floor, where we'd entered, and called out to me. "There's a strange suitcase packed with some cheap-ass women's clothes. Looks like she's headed on a cruise. Where *are* they?"

I began to wonder if they were still here, hiding. It felt like we were the bears returning home and finding signs of Goldilocks. Only I did not want to catch the lovers—and they didn't want to be found. I had to get Ally out of there. As we drove home, I realized it was time. Ally could *not* see me accept this behavior. If she did, what kind of a man would she marry? She was only seventeen, wise beyond her years after witnessing a dad with questionable morals. I realized Ally had faced the facts about her father long ago. Now, she demanded I do the same.

Lesson 17—Be Honest

"You have to divorce Dad. Mom, he's a jerk. Everyone knows it," Ally said. "You never tolerated dishonesty with us kids."

I was surprised to learn that she would be comfortable with a divorce. Society frowns upon divorced families. I'd assumed that kids want their parents to stay together. But she was right. I'd taught my children to be honest. It had been rare for the kids to lie, but any infraction had been met with a stiff penalty. It was time to face the facts. I no longer needed to stay married to Sergei over custody of Ally. He was a habitual cheater, and I couldn't change him. His dishonesty had been apparent over the years, but *my* problem was not being honest with myself. I had initially stayed with him to protect Ally. Later, we stayed together to nurture her promising tennis career. We shared a dream. But as the dream waned and she grew older, I realized she was safe now. I could let go.

The truth was that our marriage was never going to work. I wanted Sergei to be exclusive, but he couldn't. He wanted me to accept him as he was, and I refused. We were both unhappy. I had to be strong, set an example for Ally, and be a woman she could respect. I had to set Sergei free. I needed to be free. Thanks for the assist, Ally.

The next day, I scheduled an appointment with my Florida divorce attorney. That little voice had told me to be prepared—there *would* be a next time. The papers were there, waiting. Before this latest episode, I hadn't been sure I would follow through. I thought I could change Sergei and we'd grow old together. But on the phone, I told the attorney the time had come.

It had been easy to figure out who this other woman was. Sergei had frequently driven to Miami during the last few months to "give lessons" to the son of a Russian woman he'd met at a local tournament. I noticed now that his Facebook account had recently been updated with recommendations for her real estate listings for cheap property in Sunny Isles. By the time I met with my attorney to pick up the papers, Sergei had posted cruise photos with the Russian woman. He'd never posted a photo of me, his wife, on his Facebook account, but now this! Seeing which supposed friends "liked" his posts was interesting. I will never forget who they were. The truth hurt. That horrible feeling was back; once again, I was frozen. But this time, it was different. I would not be calling this Russian woman to learn the details. I didn't care. It was finally over.

Seeing posted cruise photos indicated that Sergei had returned to dry land with Wi-Fi service. I drove to the condo late that night and banged on the door. No response. Both of their cars were in the driveway. I called him by phone and demanded he come outside and speak with me.

"How could you do this to Ally?" I asked as we stood in the center of the dark cul-de-sac.

"What's *your* problem?" he asked in a menacing voice.

"My problem is you. It's enough that you've cheated on me for years and broken all vows and trust. But now our daughter knows. You are a married man who took another woman on a cruise! And posted pictures! My God! How stupid are you? I feel sorry for you. She's lost all respect for you. Someday, you'll wish you had our life together with Ally back. You lived a lie, but your truth has set *me* free." I held up the divorce papers. "What time are you available tomorrow to meet me at a notary's office?"

He seemed taken aback for once, not realizing I would or could take this final step so quickly. There was no time for me to cool off so he could back-channel his way into the marriage again, like before. He had no choice but to agree. I took a vacation day from work. The next morning, it took three stops at various banks searching for a notary who would sign off on the papers. My hands shook on the steering wheel; I worried I'd never be free of this man. But my lucky number three was a charm. There was a notary at the third bank. I drove the notarized papers to the attorney and headed home to await our June court date. I was almost free.

CHAPTER 18

My True Loves

Moana always knew she was different. With her grandmother's encouragement, she bravely followed a calling to the sea to protect what she held most dear—her people. By choosing that risky path into the unknown, Moana reached her full potential as a leader.

"Will you accept a collect call from an inmate at the Miami-Dade Correctional Facility?"

"Uh, yes?" I wondered if this was a spam call and I should've hung up. Then Sergei's voice came over the line.

"Deb, I only have a few minutes. Can you help me get lawyer? I need to get out of this place."

I hadn't heard from him much since the divorce more than a year ago. "Why don't you call your girlfriend?" I asked.

"She not my girlfriend." Apparently, Sergei had been arrested for stalking his former girlfriend, the Russian real estate agent—the one in the cruise photos. He'd placed a tracking device on the used Mercedes SUV he'd given her.

"Why don't you call Lina? She lives locally."

"I don't want my daughter to know. It's embarrassing," he said. "Deb, you are the only one I can call. You know me."

My anger toward him had softened over time, and I decided to help bail him out. But we could never be more than friends.

"Kids don't believe me when I tell them I'm not sad about you and Dad being divorced," Ally said. "He wasn't around much when I was growing up. And when he was, he was screaming half the time. Life is much easier without him. I'm glad you guys met and made me." Her eyes danced, crinkling in the corners like Sergei's. "But it was clear he wouldn't be your happily ever after. And you seem really happy now without him."

One look at Ally eased the heartache Sergei had caused me. My mind wandered back to another time. A time before I'd started arguing with Sergei and before the communication issues began, even if Sergei's English was more limited. A time when I trusted him completely. When I saw only the good in him. That time had only lasted for a moment. Before Betsy. Before Natasha. Before the cruise photos.

But Ally was right; I was much happier since the divorce. A weight had been lifted. He'd been my responsibility since I'd first helped him settle in America. My project. But no longer. I was free.

"What do you do with all your time while I'm at school, besides caring for Beanie?" Ally asked. She was in college now—a member of the Clemson University tennis team.

"Besides work, I work *out* evenings and weekends," I said. "I got a bike and signed up for fitness classes. And I think I'll go back to school and earn a doctorate. I've always loved being in the classroom. Maybe I'll retire early and teach part-time at the college level again."

"I'll race you. Let's see who gets their degree first," Ally said.

Ally won, but only by one semester.

"Hey, it's Tuesday. Are you riding your bike to lunch?" Hadley asked on her daily call.

"Yep, heading to Panera for my Pick Two." I rode to the restaurant three times a week; each round trip was fifteen miles. With the kids all grown and having retired early at sixty-one, I was able to invest a lot more time in myself.

"You gave a speech by that name years ago," Hadley said. "Pick Two."

I remembered. Back in Ohio, I'd been invited to offer leadership tips for how to reach the top as part of a United Way lunch-and-learn series attended by hundreds of women. It was my first all-female audience since I'd addressed the delegates at Girls' State during high school long ago. This time, it was a mix of stay-at-home moms and professional women.

"You used quotes from *The Velveteen Rabbit*," Hadley said.

"Real isn't how you are made; it's a thing that happens to you." I'd wanted to explain that executive women were genuine and approachable. And to show that any woman could be a leader—at any level, including by volunteering or raising their children.

Success requires focus. To excel at something, you must have the courage to focus. "Pick Two" was the name of the strategy I described to the women. I suggested choosing two items to focus on from the following list: family (however they defined it), friends, career, and self. My advice was to pick two areas and focus on those parts of their lives. Alternatively, people could choose to enjoy a wonderfully balanced life across all four areas. But if they wanted to achieve *greatness* in one or two categories, like becoming a renowned chef, athlete, musician, or leader, my theory was that the peanut butter approach wouldn't work. Their efforts would be spread too thin. Having focus doesn't mean completely ignoring the remaining two areas, I told the women; top female leaders certainly perform all four. But to be *great* at something, to achieve the highest levels of success, it was best to focus on one or two.

For me, it was family and work. I gave up spending time on myself—no massages or appointments to get my nails done. No "me time" to read the latest novel or binge-watch television. I averaged about six hours of sleep a night during the busiest years. I defined my family as my three kids, and rightly or wrongly, I largely ignored my husbands. I also stopped making time for friends. I sacrificed time with my neighbors, sorority sisters, and high school friends. I spent those extra few hours daily with my kids and working on things like developing presentations for CEOs. As Ally had named me, I was *Worker Bear*.

"That's a great quote from *The Velveteen Rabbit* about becoming real. And a lot has happened to you recently. *That's* for real," Hadley said.

She was right. A lot had happened. Mom suffered a massive stroke a few weeks after I retired from corporate life. She wanted to move to Florida with me for her recovery, where I helped care for her and her dog, Snowy. They stayed for a year before Mom wanted to return to Indiana to be near Dad's grave. I could have never given Mom (or Snowy) the amount of attention they needed if I'd been working.

Sergei helped me with Mom's moves from Indiana to Florida and back again, cheerfully driving the truck and lifting her heavy furniture. He was merely helping a friend, like when I bailed him out of jail. Nothing more. Now and then, I needed to remind him that we were better as friends than as a married couple. He sometimes forgot, like a few years after the divorce, when he got down on his knee, produced a new ring, and proposed out of the blue. Sometimes it's difficult for him to respect my boundaries, but it's easier now that he's back in Russia full-time and has another girlfriend or two. We still wish each other happy birthday: *S dnem rozhdeniya.*

My kids will always be part of my Pick Two, but letting go of Sergei and my executive position allowed me to pick another area of focus. I chose myself. Four years after divorcing Sergei, I completed a doctorate in business and my daughters attended my graduation. Mom proudly introduces me to her friends in the Indiana retirement center as "Dr. Miller." I teach online management and marketing courses part-time to MBA students worldwide and even have some undergrad students from my alma mater, Purdue.

Hadley earned an MBA at Cambridge. She later married a classmate, a British-American guy, and they live in Seattle with my first grandchild. Hadley has a great job in marketing research at Google. Tyler has a law degree from Columbia and is a patent litigator in Manhattan—precisely what he planned when he was ten. Ally earned a marketing degree and a master's while on a tennis scholarship at Clemson. After graduation, she launched a career in sports marketing, working for

Forget the Fairy Tale and Find Your Happiness

the Cleveland Cavaliers organization. Even though I led large global teams, raising three happy and successful kids has been my greatest leadership success.

Looking back, I think that simple Pick Two message does a pretty good job of summing up how I lived much of my life. Initially, I believed the classic fairy tale—that my prince would take care of me and deliver my happily ever after. But I left that traditional princess path, went all in for my organizations, and reached the vice president level at several Fortune 500 companies. I loved the work my teammates and I created professionally. I became financially secure, which allowed me to retire early and freed me to focus on myself and whatever I wanted in life.

I'd also picked and then gave up two princes. Some might conclude that meant I'd been unlucky at love—but not me. Even though Scott didn't deliver on my girlhood expectations for a prince, he showed me I *could* be loved, and our split motivated me to take charge of my kids' futures. Sergei turned out to be a less-than-ideal partner; what doesn't kill you makes you stronger. But he also made me feel alive again after my first marriage failed, and he opened my eyes to a world beyond Indiana. I remembered the independent young girl I'd been before taking society's traditional princess path.

Encouraged by the examples of my grandmothers, two single moms who worked and cared for their children during the Great Depression, I found happiness and success. Raising children has always been my goal. *They* are my true loves, my happily ever after. I picked them instead of a prince. Only I picked three. Well, four, if you count my little Beanie.

The phone rang one morning. I hoped it wasn't a FaceTime call. I dreaded those impromptu video sessions. After all those years of waking up early for kids and racing to work, I enjoyed sleeping in. I liked to lounge in my pajamas for a while. Gone were the days of eating a cold, hard granola bar in the car while conducting a conference call on my commute to work. These days, it was warm oatmeal with blueberries and hot tea while admiring my beautifully landscaped Florida backyard and the sparkling water in the pool.

"Hi, Mom. Have you started packing for Seattle yet?" Hadley, my early bird, asked. Luckily, it was a regular telephone call.

"I've been packing the house for months, but if you mean my bags, not yet . . ."

"I ran across a quote in one of the baby cards we've received for Bee," she interrupted. "Maybe you can help me create something artsy with it for the nursery when you move out here. It's by Goethe, about the gifts a parent can give a child. I took a screenshot. Here it is."

She read the quote to me: "There are two things parents should give their children—roots and wings. Roots to give them bearing and a sense of belonging, but also wings to help free them from constraints and prejudices and give them other ways to travel (or rather, to fly)."

For a moment, I imagined the poster that had been taped to my college dorm room wall with the same message.

"Mom," Hadley said. "That's what you've given *us*. I want to do the same for Bee."

A warm feeling came over me. A vision realized. Roots, but especially wings—this is what I'd wanted for myself long ago and had vowed to give to my children.

Forget the Fairy Tale and Find Your Happiness

Having wings means being free to make choices. I hoped my grown children would choose me. I'd left my parents at the curb when I went to college. I'd felt that's what they wanted—to finish their obligation as parents. Mom and I got along great when she became a grandmother, but my kids and I have always had a strong connection. We share roots no matter where we all live. Tyler consults me for occasional financial advice and calls to discuss our shared passions in the latest political and sports news. Ally and I vacation together, and she regularly updates me on her jet-setter life. I get to follow her on social media—as long as I don't post any comments. Hadley and I spoke daily, and she let me into the room for the birth of my first grandchild. She and her husband even asked me to cut the cord. When the pandemic hit right after, I decided to sell my beautiful home in Florida and relocate to Seattle to help Hadley, a working mom with a demanding job. I know a thing or two about the difficulty of balancing work and family. Being nearby, I'll be able to establish a strong tie with the next generation and enjoy my granddaughter Bee, our new little princess.

There are many important moments in life. I passed out and nearly died after my car spun out of control on black ice long ago. Instead, I went on to surpass the achievements of my corporate role model, my dad. Dad had been a workaholic who largely left the work of raising kids to Mom. I chose to make time for my kids *and* the work journey while having fun along the way. If you can, why not take your kids to Europe or ride an elephant in India and rappel the Great Wall of China while traveling for work? My sense of adventure and love of learning continues to open doors. I've recently taken up hiking and set a goal to visit all the national parks. Freedom.

Deb Miller

Lesson 18—Be Yourself

I was married for a combined thirty-five years of my life, and even though it's been years since my divorce, it still feels weird to think of myself as single. I chose to continue wearing my wedding ring after I divorced. Being different by breaking society's norms is not always easy. When strangers see my ring, they inevitably inquire about my husband. When I explain I'm divorced, they apologize but can't help nervously glancing back at the ring. Some wonder why I don't put it on my right hand. They don't understand that I no longer feel the need to follow traditions. Besides, its unique diagonal design only works on my left hand.

I've noticed that some people look at a woman differently if they think she's single. Wives may assume she's looking for a husband (I'm not), and perhaps even theirs (I would never). Some men believe that a single woman is shopping for a male companion (nope) and maybe even them (zero interest). In addition to the annoying questions about my ring, I'm reminded that society places a financial penalty on being single during tax time.

It had been easy to stop wearing Scott's wedding band, but it took me months to converse with people about our divorce. Scott was my first love, and our engagement ring symbolizes that love. Today, that ring is right where it should be: in Hadley's care as a family heirloom. It's alongside the ring I inherited from Mama Dell, now designated for her namesake, my granddaughter, Beatrice *Eloise* Edwards—Bee.

This ring, the one still on my finger, is different. I don't see Sergei when I look at this ring; I see myself. It's unusual, one of a kind. Bold and strong. Half gold and half silver, elegantly and seamlessly blending like the different parts of my life. The large center stone represents my family, surrounded by smaller glittering diamonds that remind me of each of my kids and the grandkids to come. This ring is a part of *me*. Wearing it gives me joy, and I love the life that it represents. Someday, it will belong to Ally. Maybe she'll make some jewelry out of it to honor her own life.

I still *feel* married—married to my family, the way I define it. My kids don't care whether I still wear the ring. Tyler reminded me, "You always told us just to be yourself." As I've aged, I've decided to take my own advice. I've realized I don't need to worry about what society thinks about wedding rings or anything else. After all, society's expectations led me to believe in a fairy tale that wasn't the best fit for my family or me. A princess should wear a slipper that fits. It's the same with the ring.

CHAPTER 19

Mirror, Mirror on the Wall

*M**ulan understood that society expected her to follow a traditional path for a woman. However, she chose a different way to serve her family. Eventually, her reflection would show that she'd become a courageous warrior, won the hearts of the people, and found her happiness.*

The smell of my hot buttered popcorn wafted upstairs and proved irresistible to my youngest daughter, Ally. As she plopped down on the couch, I instinctively moved to make room for her.

"I hope you've packed your umbrella for your move to the Pacific Northwest," Ally said, joining me to watch the last few minutes of Disney's *Brave*.

"Shhh. Better than snow. The rain never bothered me anyway," I whispered, engrossed in the movie. I was glad to have had Ally's company during the pandemic. After my cross-country move, I'd miss having moments like this with her.

"Wrong movie, Elsa... er, Mom. Although I never saw *this* Disney movie," she said.

Hearing that, I felt obligated to catch her up on the parts she'd missed. As usual, she didn't want to listen to my commentary. Ally had recently graduated from college—the time in your life when you think you know everything.

"Just let me listen! It looks pretty easy to figure out," she declared.

I couldn't resist sharing my theory. "I think the big bear will turn into a long-lost prince, kinda like Beauty and the Beast, and Merida will marry him. The other three candidates were duds."

Ally stuck her hand into the bottom of the popcorn bowl, searching for a few extra buttery pieces, and replied, deadpan, "She's on her own, Mom. No one is coming."

"No way. Disney will send a prince. They always do," I assured her, handing over the bowl and wishing I hadn't eaten so many pieces drenched in butter, the ones she loves.

As the movie wound down, Merida seemed to be aligned with Ally. No prince had come (yet) to save the day. I could not believe Disney would fail to produce a prince to rescue the damsel in distress. Out of nowhere, I began to laugh hysterically. The kind of laughter you can't stop when the tears come, and later, you can't explain what was so funny. Was I laughing at Ally's confidence? Or was it nervous laughter out of fear that she might be right? Tears streamed down my face. Could it be true that no prince was coming? Sixty-plus years of the princess path had programmed me otherwise. I clung to the belief that Merida's happily ever after would still come in the form of a prince.

The movie credits rolled. Still laughing about Ally's confident prediction but also believing she had to be wrong, I proclaimed, "Disney will bring the prince—*in the credits*! He's coming!"

My brain was catching up. Slowly, I realized how silly I must've sounded, how stupid I'd been... and not only tonight. Through my hysterical tears, I tried to reconcile the end of this movie with my inner beliefs about the princess path—how a woman needed a man to sweep in and rescue her, or at least go along with her, to the happily ever after. But I didn't have a prince anymore—yet *I* was happy.

Ally tried to snap me out of it and bring me into the twenty-first century. "Mom, what year was this movie made?" She googled it in seconds. "Eight years ago, Mom. Disney got it by then. Girls don't *need* a prince. They're optional."

"How do you know that?" I implored, still laughing through my hysteria, in tears over this epic breakthrough and my daughter's clarity and candor. But most importantly, I genuinely wanted to know her answer to this vital question. How did she know that girls don't need a prince? This was contrary to my belief system—to the princess path.

"*You*, above everyone else, should already know this," Ally said.

Lesson 19—Be Happy

At that moment, I understood today's girls. These modern-day princesses don't need a prince to solve their problems or make them happy. Disney understood that. But more importantly, Ally did too. And even better, she saw me as an example of this message. I was her mother, and she told me I'd somehow taught her this truth without learning it for myself... until now.

"Mom, relax. You don't have to marry me off. You'll have grandchildren someday. I'll find the right guy when I'm ready. I'm not sitting around waiting for a perfect prince with a glass slipper to save the day. That's up to me. Forget what society told you. It's irrelevant. Mulan solved her problems. Moana. Merida. Mom, you did too! I got this. It's my life."

Forget glass slippers. With an endorsement like that from my daughter, I felt like I'd just cracked open the whole glass ceiling. If girls like Ally can forge their own way and forget the Prince Charming fairy tale, it will save them a lot of future heartache.

"Seriously, Mom, you've always shown us that anything is possible. How great life can be. 'I just want you to be happy,' you always told us. Well, I'm in charge of my happiness. I am perfectly capable of choosing my own path. You did."

And there it was. My life felt complete. My kids got it. And now, the woman looking back at me in the mirror did too.

Epilogue

There's a path for every princess. Every person. Billions of paths. My kids already knew that. They assumed I did too, and gave me credit for leading a path-breaking life. I discovered that the traditional compass didn't lead to happiness. And that I didn't need a prince to take me there. Disney must have learned this too—the central relationship in *Brave* is between mother and daughter, and in *Frozen*, it's between sisters. Moana gains strength from her grandmother. Girl power!

It seems obvious now, but I had to find my way. Like the princess characters, it has taken time for me to evolve and catch up to today's young girls, who dream of endless possibilities and know that true happiness comes from charting their own path.

It was one of those beautiful days when you wanted to leave the car windows down to feel the warm, salty ocean breeze. I'd come a long way from that wintry day in January 2000 when I veered off course and nearly lost my life. What doesn't kill you...

I paused in the driveway of my lovely Florida home to enjoy one of my last looks at the thick, woody bougainvillea vine gracefully arching over the front door. The plant had been spectacular in the spring, but now only a few paperlike fuchsia bracts remained amidst the dark green leaves, concealing the sharp thorns beneath. The phone rang, snapping me out of my long gaze, and I pushed the button on the car's dashboard to take the call.

"Hey, Mom," Hadley said. "I know you haven't decided yet if you're driving or flying, but I wanted to get an ETA if you drive cross-country."

I smiled, recalling how often I'd been asked the "Are we there yet?" question by young voices sitting in the back seat. "Let me check." I touched Hadley's address on the Tesla screen and reported, "If I drive, it will take about a week. There are a few different routes, and I'd need to charge now and then. Don't worry. Help is on the way."

"I honestly don't know how you did it with three kids." She sounded like she was about to cry. "I can't tell you how much it means to Nick and me for you to move out here to help with Bee."

"She and I will have a ball!"

"Me too!" Hadley added, not wanting to be excluded from potential adventure.

"We always do. It will 'Bee' awesome."

I liked living in Florida, but I'd considered moving to Washington at some point to be closer to my grandchild. The pandemic solidified my plans—I wanted to help the two young parents who were trying to work from home while caring for a baby. I sold my house and donated many of my belongings. The remainder were already headed west in several portable containers.

"Ha-ha. I see what you're doing there," Hadley said. "It will 'Bee' fun. I wish Beanie could've come with you," she added, knowing how much I missed my little guy. We'd recently laid him to rest due to an incurable illness.

"Me too," I said softly, glancing over at his blanket, which was still in the front seat beside me. I imagined his nose pressed against the window, ready to go anywhere. Perhaps it was time to start thinking about getting a new dog.

As my car entered the freeway, I picked up speed and turned up the volume. Elsa, the princess from *Frozen*, was singing "Let It Go." I felt fierce and free. Finding your happily ever after can do that for you.

Acknowledgments

I would like to thank Peggy Orenstein, author of *Cinderella Ate My Daughter*, for inspiring the Disney princess epigraph framework for this memoir.

I may forget the fairy tale, but I will always remember and appreciate the undying encouragement and support of my editor, Julie Artz.

About the Author

Photo credit: Ally Miller

Deb Miller's life is a tapestry of adventure and achievement, weaving together experiences from her small-town Indiana roots to business opportunities in Red Square and beyond. Her job as a hardworking Fortune 500 executive led to her rappelling the Great Wall and riding elephants in India, all while remaining a devoted mom. Now a part-time marketing professor, Dr. Miller cherishes the opportunity to learn from her global students as well as her beloved children and grandchildren. Deb resides in an enchanted forest outside of Seattle, where the landscaping projects are endless and enjoyable.

For more information visit forgetthefairytale.NET

Looking for your next great read?

We can help!

Visit www.shewritespress.com/next-read
or scan the QR code below for a list
of our recommended titles.

She Writes Press is an award-winning
independent publishing company founded to
serve women writers everywhere.